FELTED WOOL FASHIONS

FELTED WOOL FASHIONS
Making New Styles from Old Knits

Vivian Peritts

STERLING

New York / London
www.sterlingpublishing.com

Prolific Impressions Production Staff:
Editor in Chief: Mickey Baskett
Copy Editor: Phyllis Mueller
Graphics: Cindy Gorder
Styling: Lenos Key
Photography: Jerry Mucklow, Joel Tressler
Administration: Jim Baskett

Every effort has been made to insure that the information presented is accurate. Since we have no control over physical conditions, individual skills, or chosen tools and products, the publisher disclaims any liability for injuries, losses, untoward results, or any other damages which may result from the use of the information in this book. Thoroughly read the instructions for all products used to complete the projects in this book, paying particular attention to all cautions and warnings shown for that product to ensure their proper and safe use.

Library of Congress Cataloging-in-Publication Data

Peritts, Vivian.
  Felted wool fashions : making new styles from old knits / Vivian Peritts.
       p. cm.
  Includes index.
  ISBN-13: 978-1-4027-5310-7
  ISBN-10: 1-4027-5310-1
1. Felt work. 2. Felting. 3. Clothing and dress--Remaking. I. Title.

TT849.5.P47 2007
746'.0463--dc22

                                        2007017620

2 4 6 8 10 9 7 5 3 1

Published by Sterling Publishing Co., Inc.
387 Park Avenue South, New York, NY 10016
© 2008 by Prolific Impressions, Inc.
Distributed in Canada by Sterling Publishing
c/o Canadian Manda Group, 165 Dufferin Street,
Toronto, Ontario, Canada M6K 3H6
Distributed in the United Kingdom by GMC Distribution Services,
Castle Place, 166 High Street, Lewes, East Sussex, England BN7 1XU
Distributed in Australia by Capricorn Link (Australia) Pty. Ltd.
P.O. Box 704, Windsor, NSW 2756, Australia

Printed in China
All rights reserved

ISBN-13: 978-1-4027-5310-7
ISBN-10: 1-4027-5310-1

For information about custom editions, special sales, premium and corporate purchases, please contact Sterling Special Sales Department at 800-805-5489 or specialsales@sterlingpub.com.

About the Author

Vivian Peritts is a designer, crafter, and author who has written several books and created over 100 patterns. Her designs have appeared in numerous national publications, and she has taught many workshops at national trade shows and is a frequent guest on national cable television shows.

She lives in Marietta, Georgia with her husband, Virgil, two dogs, and a parrot.

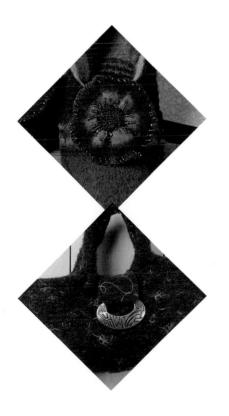

Acknowledgments

Vivian Peritts thanks Linda Baird for all her help in preparing the manuscript.

She would also like to thank the following companies for their generous contributions of products for use in this book:

For Buttons and Closures:
JHB International, Inc., 1955 South Quince St., Denver, Colorado 80231, www.buttons.com

For Ultra Solvy™ Heavy Water Soluble Stabilizer and Thread:
Sulky of America, 3113 Broadpoint Drive, Punta Gorda, FL 33983, www.sulky.com

For Cutting Tools, Mats, Rulers, and Pliers:
Fiskars® Brands Inc., 2537 Daniels Street, Madison, WI 53718-6772

Table of Contents

54

68

82

90

98

Wool Felting is my way of Recycling Creatively

*m*y discovery and experimentation with wool felting or "boiled wool" began with my desire to recycle old wool sweaters. "Surely there must be some life left in these old, but lovely, wool sweaters I had stored away." I thought. When I did some research about what felted wool was and how it was done, I decided to experiment with my old sweaters.

This is the jacket that started it all. With those first wool sweaters that I washed and dried, I cut apart the good pieces of fabric and pieced them into a jacket.

So I washed them and dried them. When I took that first wool sweater out of the clothes dryer I knew I had the beginnings of something exciting. I had created felted wool and realized I could use that wool fabric for creating new and restyled wearables.

And you can too. Your old wool sweaters are so full of warm winter memories. If you're like me, when the weather starts to get a little nippy, you open your cedar chest or storage closet and out come all those special treasures. When you put one on, you snuggle right up to the past. Holiday smells, family gatherings, your first love, bonfires—they all live on in the wool. That's why it's so hard to give away these sweaters, even ones that don't really fit anymore. You overlook the fact that they have holes and stains, and you don't notice that they look hopelessly out of date—just so you can keep your memories and go through this ritual one more time.

Now you don't have to throw those old wool sweaters away—recycle them! Why not take all those wonderful woolen memories and combine them into new memorable outfits. Restyle them! This book is filled with ideas for recycling and restyling your (or someone else's) castoff wool sweaters by turning them into felted woolen fabric and cutting and combining them in interesting ways.

You'll learn everything you need to get started, including how to select sweaters for recycling and a simple technique for felting. You'll see piecing and cutting techniques for felted sweaters, machine and hand embroidery for stitching and embellishing, and sewing techniques for felted fabric. I'll show you how to make fabulous felted flowers and three kinds of buttonholes, and how to attach all kinds of buttons.

There are projects galore. Coverings like capes, vests, shawls, and jackets—even a dog sweater. Cozy, comfy slippers. A variety of accessories, including scarves, hats, tote bags, and purses. Jewelry, too. Useful, wonderful, colorful one-of-a-kind creations. Have fun making them!

Vivian Peritts

This is the back of my first felted wool jacket. The simple design includes pieces of six sweaters, machine stitching, hand embroidery, and a single button closure.

Gather Your Supplies

*t*his section shows and describes the supplies and tools you'll need to create your felted fashions, starting with wool sweaters and basic sewing tools and progressing to more specialized tools and materials for trimming and embellishing.

Start with a Wool Sweater

$y$our new felted fashions start with knitted sweaters—100% wool is best. You can start your search for sweaters in your own closets and storage areas. Chances are you have sweaters you or other family members have outgrown. Or sweaters that are stained or torn or damaged by moths. Perhaps these are sentimental favorites you haven't been willing to part with. Lucky you! This is your chance to recycle them and wear them again.

If you have purged your closets of sweaters that don't fit or are damaged, you probably donated them to a charity thrift shop. Thrift shops are the best place to look for sweaters for felting—you'll find them in every shape, color, and size. They're inexpensive (a few dollars each) so go ahead and buy a lot of them—you'll have lots of material for your projects. You'll be giving these sweaters a second life and recycling something that might otherwise be discarded, and your purchases benefit the charities.

Since size doesn't matter, check out men's and children's sweaters as well. Choose sweaters in colors you love. Sweaters with knitted patterns, wool embroidery, and multi-colored designs like stripes and argyles will add interest and texture to your felted fashions. Don't overlook sweaters with holes in them. (I call these "openings of opportunity".) If the color is too good to pass up, you can work around the holes. Small holes will disappear in the felting process, and you can mend larger holes with wool yarn before felting or cover any holes that remain after felting with embellishments, trims, or pockets.

I have used knitted wool sweaters to make all the projects in this book, but you can also felt 100% woven wool fabric or use "boiled wool" fabrics or jackets. Boiled wool is what its name implies—wool that has been shrunk by hot water. Use the same felting process for wool fabric and boiled wool that you use for sweaters.

- Choose 100% wool sweaters. Avoid blends.

- Choose sweaters and fabrics labeled "Dry Clean Only."

- If a garment has appliques or embroidery, check to see if those are 100% wool as well. If they aren't, remove them before felting.

This shows a vest before and after washing and drying. It already had machine embroidery on it when I purchased it from a thrift store. Washing it did not compromise the snowflake embroidery.

Cutting Tools

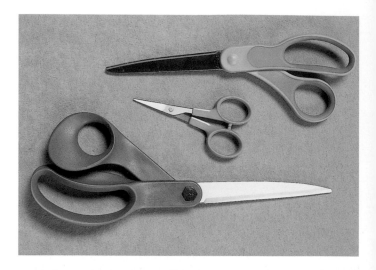

SCISSORS

Fabric scissors with sharp blades make precise, clean-edged cuts—even through multiple layers. Scissors with longer blades provide more efficient cutting; shorter blades provide more control. Contoured offset handles reduce hand fatigue and make cutting easier on flat surfaces. Choose a pair that feels good in your hand; for additional comfort, try a pair with padded handles.

Small craft scissors are useful for snipping threads and yarns and for precise cutting in tight areas, such as trimming close to stitching after joining fabrics with machine embroidery. Their small size provides more control.

ROTARY CUTTERS

Rotary cutters have a sharp metal wheel for cutting mounted on a plastic handle. Faster than scissors, they can cut thick and thin fabrics and make straight or curved cuts. When the blade becomes dull, it can be replaced. Rotary cutters come in different sizes. Choose one that feels comfortable in your hand.

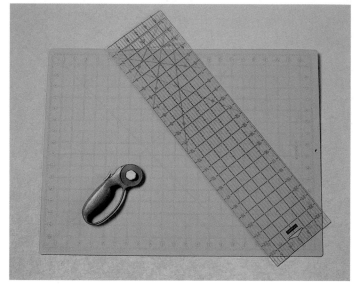

CUTTING MAT

You'll need a self-healing cutting mat to protect your work surface when you use rotary cutters. It's a good idea to buy the largest one you can afford.

RULER

For making straight cuts, use a ruler with rotary cutters. A transparent one will allow you to see the fabric as you cut, and the markings will allow you to align the ruler with markings on the fabric or on your cutting mat.

Sewing Tools & Supplies

SEWING MACHINE

Although many projects can be created with hand stitches, machine stitching is the quickest, easiest way to piece felted fabrics, sew seams, and add decorative stitching.

Machine stitches that give the best results are overlock stitches. Most machines can make some form of an overlock stitch. I like to use a 1/4" seam allowance for most seams, and I use overlock stitches for joining overlapped pieces of wool. If your machine doesn't have an overlock stitch, use a zig-zag stitch.

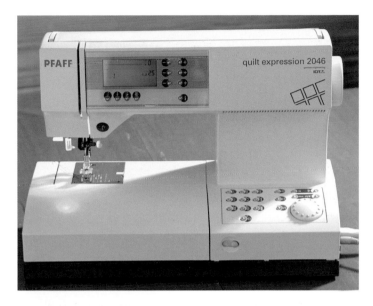

THREAD

Regular sewing thread—the kind that comes on spools in a huge variety of colors—is readily available at fabric, craft, and department stores. Use it for machine stitching and hand sewing tasks such as attaching trims and buttons.

FABRIC STABILIZER

When machine stitching felted wool, I always use a stabilizer. A water soluble (rinse away) stabilizer keeps the wool from stretching out of shape as you stitch and is easy to remove. It comes in packages, rolls, and bolts in various widths and lengths. Follow the manufacturer's instructions for best results.

SEAM RIPPER

You'll want to have a seam ripper to remove unwanted stitching from garments, to remove buttons from sweaters, and to remove unwanted trims from sweaters before felting.

TAPE MEASURE

A tape measure is indispensable for measuring curved surfaces (such as the body) and curved areas of patterns. Choose one made of a material that won't stretch out of shape.

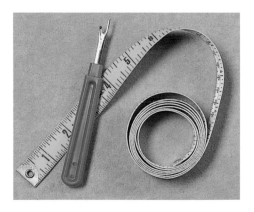

Needles for Hand Sewing

Hand sewing needles are used for basting, embroidery, and beading and for attaching buttons and trims. Choose needles for hand sewing according to the task.

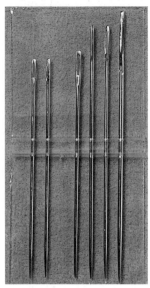

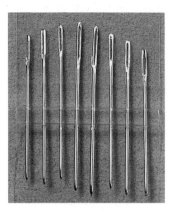

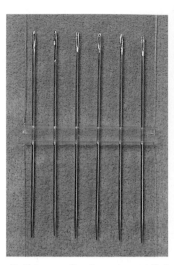

Darners are long, heavy needles with large eyes that are used for stitching with yarn. Used for finishing edges with yarn, ribbon and floss.

Tapestry needles have large eyes and blunt points that allow the needle to pass easily between the yarns in the fabric so they are ideal for stitching on knitted items. Great for doing embroidery with yarns and floss.

Beading needles are very fine needles used for sewing beads, sequins, and pearls.

Quilting needles (sometimes called *basting* needles) are long, fine needles that are good for sewing through multiple layers of fabric.

Needlenose Pliers

Needlenose pliers are great for bending, shaping, and twisting wire. They were invaluable when I was constructing the purses. I also use them for cutting wire and securing crimp beads when making jewelry. Pliers with spring action handles are self-opening and reduce hand fatigue; ones with coated handles are easier to grip.

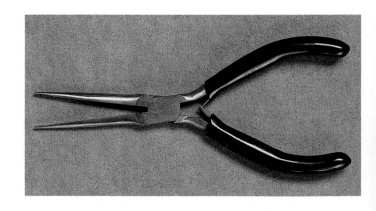

Yarns & Threads

WOOL YARNS

Wool yarns can be used for decoration before or after felting. If added before felting, the yarn will shrink along with the sweater. These are the two main types:

- **Tapestry or Persian yarn** is 3-ply 100% wool yarn that is used mainly for crewel embroidery and needlepoint. Find it in needlework stores in skeins of various lengths.

- 100% wool **knitting yarn** is used for knitting and crocheting. Find it in needlework stores and craft departments.

DECORATIVE YARNS

Yarns of all types can be used for embellishing felted wool fashions and for adding interest, color, and texture. The yarns can be any size or fiber content, and they can be textured, string, or ribbon yarns. Many are great for edging. Some are too bulky to pull through the wool but are wonderful for couching (attaching) on the surface with machine or by hand stitches. (See the Basic Techniques section for instructions.)

EMBROIDERY FLOSS

Floss is 6-ply cotton thread that comes in a pull skein in a huge range of colors. I also use **pearl (perle) cotton** embroidery thread, which comes in skeins or on balls. I use this for some of the decorative stitches and trims.

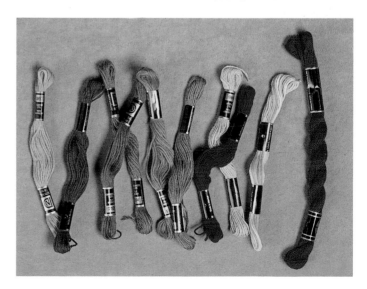

Other Embellishments

BUTTONS & CLOSURES

Buttons come in a huge variety of designs, materials, colors, and textures. They can be used on felted garments as closures, as accents, and as decorations.

To give the garment support, I like to use two buttons—a decorative button on the right side of the garment and a smaller flat button on the underside. The buttons should have the same number of holes.

Frog closures are available at fabric stores, or you can make your own from cording. Since color selection in purchased frog closures is limited, I included my technique for custom-coloring them with the instructions for the "Little Miss Jacket" project.

BEADS & BEADING WIRE

Beads add color, texture, and sparkle to felted fashions. I especially like adding them to felted wool flowers. Beads look great when combined with felted wool in necklaces and bracelets, and they can be used to make one-of-a-kind purse handles. Beads can be sewn with thread or strung on wire. The individual projects contain specific instructions for using beads.

Jewelry findings are used as closures for necklaces and bracelets. These can be found at most crafts shops or beading stores.

Miscellaneous Supplies

MARKING PENS & PENCILS

Marking pens and pencils are used to mark the placement of decorative yarns and trims before stitching, to mark the placement of buttons, and to mark buttonholes. You can also use markers to trace around pattern pieces. Choose chalk or water soluble markers, which make removable marks, for areas where you don't want the marks to show.

TRANSFER PAPER

Use transfer paper for transferring pattern markings such as darts and pattern details for embroidery.

PATTERNS

Patterns are included for all the projects in this book. Some—the smaller ones like baby shoes and flower shapes—are presented full size; larger pattern pieces are printed on grids and can be enlarged to any size. To determine how much to enlarge a pattern, consider the style of the garment and the size of the person who will be wearing it. In some instances it may be easiest to work from body measurements; other times you may wish to refer to a commercial pattern you have used before or use another garment (one you made or one you bought) as a guide.

PLASTIC TUBING

Lengths of clear vinyl tubing are used as the bases for bangle bracelets. They can be easily cut to any size and are joined with a short piece of a smaller-diameter tubing that is secured with glue.

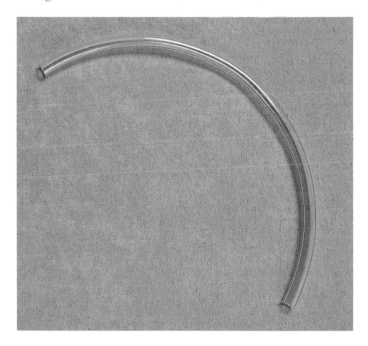

Basic Techniques

*t*his section shows you the basic techniques for felting and constructing felted garments. You'll learn about the techniques I use for finishing edges, and see how to do hand and machine stitching and embroidery and how to make three kinds of buttonholes and sew on buttons.

It is so easy to create all the wonderful fashions shown in this book. After creating the felted wool by washing and drying wool sweaters, follow my instructions for sewing your fabric into garments and adding the finishing touches.

• WASH •
• DRY •
• SEW •
• TRIM •

Creating Felted Wool

Felting is something we have all done before, though perhaps not intentionally. (Remember accidentally putting a wool garment through the washer and dryer and pulling out something smaller and denser?) Felting sweaters works much the same way. The intentional method of felting I found to be most effective is very simple. You need a regular washing machine, a clothes dryer, and some dishwashing soap or shampoo. Because the projects in this book are made by cutting up felted wool sweaters, there is no sizing or blocking involved.

Wool felting occurs when hot water and soap such as liquid dishwashing soap or shampoo are combined with the agitating action of a washing machine. Wool fibers naturally have barbs that intertwine and catch on each other; heat, soap, and friction from agitation cause the fibers to become more intertwined, making the sweater smaller and more compact and dense. How a sweater will *felt* depends on the size of yarn it was made with and the stitches used.

STEP 1: WASH

Place one or two sweaters in a washing machine set on the lowest water level. Because agitation and friction are important to the felting process, it's a good idea to felt more than one item at a time to increase the friction. Add hot water and one tablespoon of liquid dishwashing soap or shampoo. Wash.

TIP: If you only have one item to felt, throw in an old towel or a few old t-shirts to create more friction.

STEP 2: DRY

After the washing and spinning cycles are finished, place the sweaters in a dryer set on high heat and tumble until dry. *Note: Some felters prefer to air dry their felted wool, rather than using the dryer. Honestly, I can't tell the difference.* I use the dryer because I typically felt many sweaters at one time, and I don't have enough flat surfaces to lay them on. Repeat the process to shrink the sweater even more. The more you do this, the bulkier the wool becomes. Successful felting has occurred when the knitting stitches in the garment are no longer visible.

Piecing Felted Wool

Since sweaters shrink when they are felted, it is hard to cut enough pieces from a single sweater to make an adult-size garment, although you can make children's clothes and accessories like tote bags, handbags, scarves, and slippers from a single sweater. Piecing parts of sweaters to make a larger piece of fabric is one solution; so is cutting different pattern pieces from different sweaters.

Piecing felted wool for a garment will make the garment your unique creation, and combining colors and patterns is fun and the result is much more interesting than a garment made from all the same fabric. Since felted sweaters have no grainlines to worry about and stretch only minimally, you have more freedom to choose how to combine the pieces.

Here's How:

1. Cut up your felted sweaters, starting by creating large, flat pieces.
2. Lay out the pieces of felted wool, overlapping them 1/2" to make a large piece. See Fig. 1. The pieces don't have to fit together exactly (like a puzzle would, for example). Use your pattern piece as a guide for the size and shape your pieced fabric needs to be. (Fig. 2)
3. Sew the pieces together with a decorative sewing machine stitch. Always use a water soluble stabilizer to keep the fabric from stretching when you machine stitch. (A water soluble stabilizer is easy to remove from the garment after the garment is completed.)

4. When you've sewn the pieces together, trim off any excess felted fabric from uneven overlapping on the top and bottom of the pieced fabric.
5. Position the pattern piece on the fabric and cut out. ❋

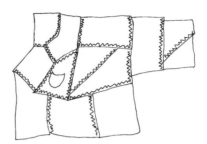

Fig. 1 - Pieces of felted sweaters arranged and stitched to make a larger piece of fabric.

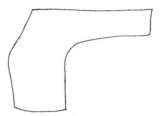

Fig. 2 - Use the pattern piece as a guide for the size and shape your pieced fabric needs to be.

Cutting Long Strips

Here's the technique I use to cut long strips of wool. Choose a sweater that does not have side seams.

1. Cut off the ribbing at the bottom of the sweater. Set it aside.
   (Fig. 1)
2. Decide how wide you want the strip to be and make a tapered cut up from the bottom of the sweater. For example, if you decide you want a strip 1" wide, cut 1" up from the bottom. (Fig. 1)
3. Begin cutting around the bottom of the sweater. Continue cutting, spiraling upward, keeping the strip the same width, until you have a strip as long as you need for your project. Trim the irregular shape at the beginning of your strip. (Fig. 2) ❋

Fig. 1 - Removing the ribbing and beginning the spiral cut.

Fig. 2 - Cutting the strip and trimming the tapered end.

Finishing Edges

After the felting has occurred, the sweater can be cut easily with scissors, and the edges will not fray or unravel. Pinking shears can be used for cutting but are not necessary. Much of the time I leave edges unfinished. **Finishing the edges** is a way of adding another decorative element to a garment. Here are two hand stitches I often use for finishing edges.

OVERCAST STITCH

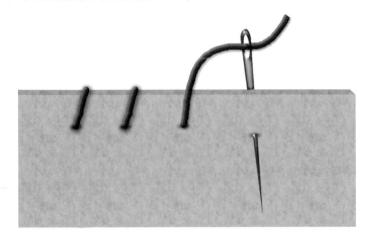

Keep the stitches evenly spaced, approximately 1/2" apart and 1/2" long.

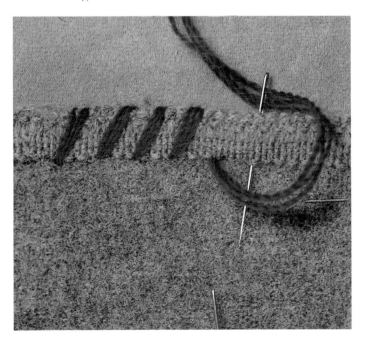

BLANKET STITCH

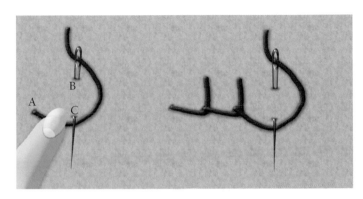

Work this stitch from left to right, keeping your stitches the same distance apart. Come up at A, hold the thread with your thumb, go down at B, and come up at C, bringing the needle tip over the thread. Carefully pull the thread into place. The bottom of the stitch will lie on the edge.

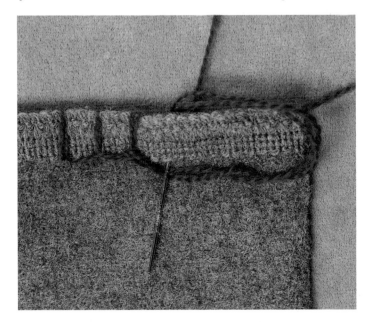

Machine Embroidery

Machine embroidery stitches can be used for piecing the
fabric together or for decoration. I like to use a water soluble
stabilizer when I machine stitch.

*Here the machine stitches are shown done on paper so that you can
better see the stitch.*

*The same machine stitches sewn on a piece
of wool so you can see the actual look.*

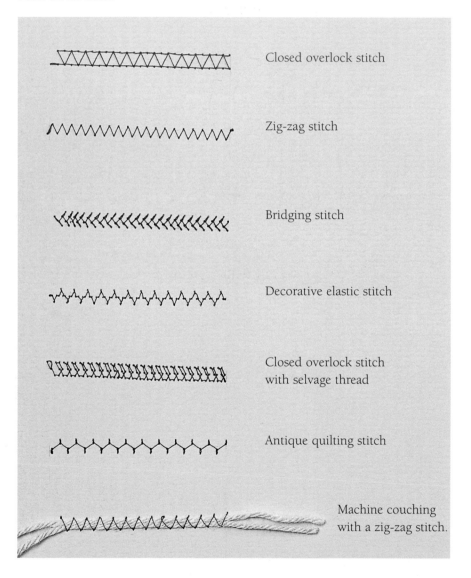

Closed overlock stitch

Zig-zag stitch

Bridging stitch

Decorative elastic stitch

Closed overlock stitch
with selvage thread

Antique quilting stitch

Machine couching
with a zig-zag stitch.

Hand Embroidery

I often use hand embroidery stitches for embellishing. It is not necessary to use stabilizer when handstitching felted wool. In addition to the stitches below and on the following pages, you can also use the overcast stitch and blanket stitch, described and shown in the "Finishing Edges" section.

CHAIN STITCH

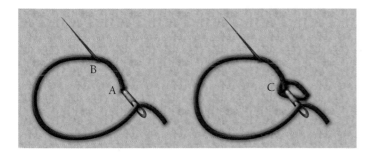

1. Come up at A. Go down to the left of A and come up at B. Loop the thread under the needle point from right to left.

2. Pull the thread through. Go down to the left of B, inserting the needle through the loop, and come up at C. Loop thread as shown in step 1.

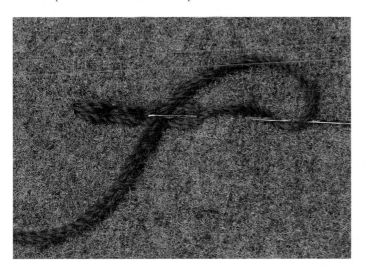

LAZY DAISY STITCH

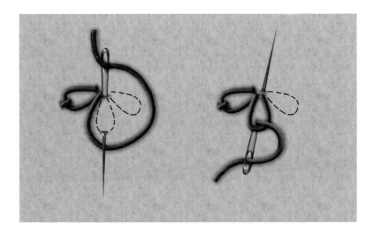

This is a variation of the chain stitch.

STEM STITCH or OUTLINE STITCH

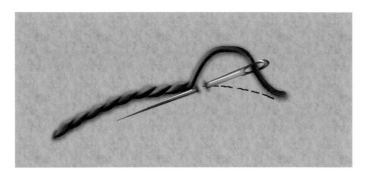

Working from left to right, bring the needle up at the end of the line to be covered. Insert the needle point a short distance ahead, bringing the point out halfway between the place of insertion and the starting place.

FRENCH KNOT

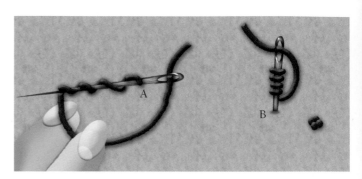

Come up at A with the needle tip pointing toward your left arm and wrap the thread four times around the needle. While holding the thread taut, turn the needle toward you, taking the needle down at B as close as you can to A. Guide the thread into the fabric and hold the knot in place until your needle is all the way through the fabric.

SINGLE CROSS STITCH

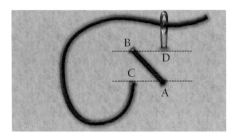

Basic Pattern: Come up at A, down at B, up at C, down at D. The stitch can be reversed so that top half slants from lower right to upper left.

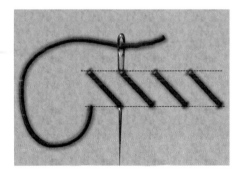

To work a row, make even, equally spaced diagonal stitches, working from bottom to top. Then go down at top left of previous stitch to make the second set of diagonal stitches and work back across the row.

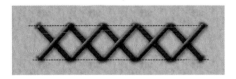

The slanting stitches in two directions form a line of Xs (crosses).

SATIN STITCH

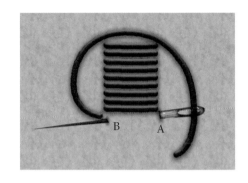

Put the needle in at A and come out at B. Pull the thread gently. Place the stitches close together, continuing to go down and come up. Keep an even edge and keep the tension tight but smooth.

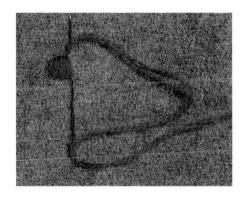

COUCHING

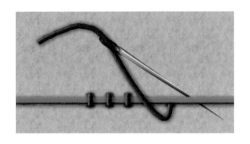

Couching is an overcast stitch made with a lighter thread to hold one or more heavier threads or yarns to the surface.

Position a piece of decorative yarn or ribbon on the surface. Using small stitches, sew over the yarn or ribbon with another piece of yarn or thread.

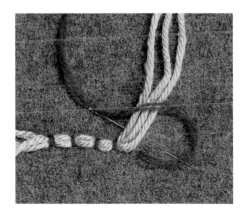

Buttonholes & Buttons

MAKING A SIMPLE BUTTONHOLE

1. Measure the width of the button.
2. Baste stitch the location of the buttonhole with a contrasting color of thread. Be exact with measurements. (Fig. 1)
3. Machine stitch around the basted buttonhole, (Fig. 2) going 1/8" above the line, sewing down to the end of the buttonhole, then 1/8" below the buttonhole, and up the side next to the basted line.
4. Cut the buttonhole along the basted line. Remove the basting threads.

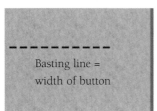

Basting line = width of button

Edge of garment

Fig. 1

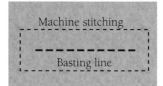

Machine stitching

Basting line

Fig. 2

MAKING A HANDSTITCHED BUTTONHOLE

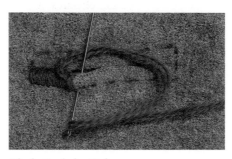

The buttonhole stitch

1. Cut a buttonhole the correct size for the width of the button. (Be careful not to make the hole too big. TIP: Practice on a scrap.) Machine or hand stitch 1/8" around the cut buttonhole. (Fig. 1)
2. Using wool yarn or cording, sew a buttonhole stitch (the blanket stitch, very closely spaced) along the top and bottom cut edges. (Fig. 2)
3. Secure both ends with a row of satin stitches. (Fig. 3)

Fig. 1

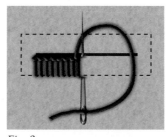

Fig. 2

Fig. 3

MAKING A BOUND BUTTONHOLE

1. Mark the placement of the buttonhole on the garment with basting thread along the buttonhole line and on both sides of the buttonhole. (Fig. 1)
2. Cut a piece of fabric (matching or contrasting) 1" wide and 1" longer than the finished length of the buttonhole.
3. With right sides out, fold the cut fabric lengthwise down the center and press lightly.
4. Lay the fabric flat. Fold the raw edges inward so they meet at the crease. (Fig. 2) Press and baste the folds in place.
5. Center the crease of the buttonhole fabric on the right side of the garment, placing it on the marked center line of the buttonhole. Baste down the center crease of the buttonhole fabric. (Fig. 3)
6. By hand or machine, stitch 1/8" from the raw edge on each side of the folded buttonhole fabric, stopping at the side basting mark. (Fig. 4) **Do not** sew across the ends.
7. On the wrong side of the garment, use a craft knife and ruler to cut an X between the two lines of stitching. (Fig. 5)

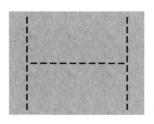

Fig. 1

Fig. 2

8. Turn the buttonhole fabric to the wrong side of the garment through the slit. (Fig. 6) Press the band flat.
9. Baste the buttonhole opening closed. (Fig. 7) Leave this basting thread in until the garment is complete.
10. Sew the fabric triangles (formed when the buttonhole was cut) to the end edges of the buttonhole fabric, being careful to not catch the garment fabric in the stitches. (Fig. 8)
11. Press, trim the edges of the buttonhole strip, and press again.

Fig. 3

Fig. 4

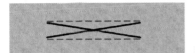

Fig.5

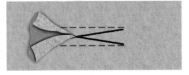

Fig. 6

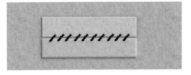

Fig. 7

Fig.8

SEWING BUTTONS

Buttons can be used as closures or as decorations. To give your garment support, use two buttons—a decorative button on the right side of the garment and a smaller flat button on the underside. The buttons should have the same number of holes; if you use a shank button, choose a two-hole button for the underside.

1. Mark the placement of the button(s).
2. Position the decorative button on the right side of the garment. Unless the button has a shank, place a toothpick or matchstick as a spacer on top of the front button so that the holes in the button are exposed. Position the flat button on the wrong side of the fabric, lining up the holes.
3. Sew the front button and the back button together through the fabric, carrying the thread over the spacer on top. (Fig. 1) Remove the spacer.
4. Bring the loose thread (the thread shank) that was over the spacer through the button —but not the fabric. Bring the threaded needle to the right side of the garment and wrap the thread end several times around the thread shank between the button and the fabric. (Fig. 2)
5. Take the needle through the fabric and secure the thread on the back of the garment. ❀

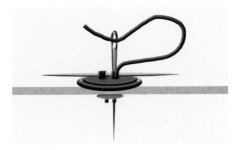

Fig. 1 - Horizontal view, showing (top to bottom) the spacer, the decorative button on the right side of the fabric, the fabric, the button on the underside.

Fig. 2 - Wrapping the thread to finish the thread shank.

Making a Garment
with Felted Wool Sweaters

When you choose felted sweaters to combine for a garment, your first consideration is selecting colors that look good together. Before you start constructing your project, however, there are other characteristics to consider, such as patterns, texture, flexibility, and thickness.

Color - Choosing sweaters that are all the same color is one way to go; choosing sweaters that are variations of one color or hue is another. You can also choose sweaters in several complementary colors. Keep in mind that some projects look better when the pieces have no color connection.

Pattern - You can use pattern as a connection for combinations, choosing sweaters with stripes, embroidery, diamonds, or flowers, for example. Wool embroidery on a wool sweater can yield beautiful results because the embroidery and the sweater all felt at the same time.

Texture - It is important to consider the texture of each felted sweater when deciding how to use it. Felted sweaters with heavy texture are good for items with a more structured look, such as handbags, vests, and jackets. Soft textures are more fluid and better suited for items that should drape and flex, like shawls, scarves, and skirts.

You can combine textures, of course, but make sure the texture is appropriate for its position on the garment. For example, soft folds are good for underarm pieces and parts that don't need support, but won't work as well for parts of a garment that require more stability, such as necklines or hat brims.

Using Patterns

After you have chosen the felted sweaters you want to use for your project, you need full size copies of your pattern pieces.

If you're using patterns from this book, in most cases you will need to enlarge the pattern to the desired size, either by sketching the pattern on gridded pattern paper or tracing paper placed over a grid or by using a photocopier. To determine how much to enlarge a pattern, it may be easiest to work from body measurements; other times you may wish to refer to a commercial pattern you have used before or use another garment (one you made or one you bought) as a guide. When you have enlarged the pieces to the desired size, cut them out.

If you're using a purchased pattern, it is a good idea to start by cutting out all the pattern pieces. If the pattern has pieces that are cut on the fold, such as the back of a vest, make a full size copy of the pattern piece so you can use it when piecing your fabric — to see the sizes you need to piece and for the placement of the pieces within the pattern section. (Fig. 1)

Hems - Since no hems are needed on felted fashions, you can cut sleeve patterns to the exact length. This also is true for the bottom hems on any garment.

Seam allowances for facings - You can cut off seam allowances for facings if you aren't using facings. There are some exceptions to this rule, though. For example, if you are making a heavy coat and the felted fabric is too lightweight. In this case, you may want to add facings, interfacing, and maybe even a lining.

Fig. 1 - Making a full size copy of a pattern piece.

Cutting Felted Fabric

Decide which sections of your sweater knits that you want to use for your garment pattern sections. Cut open sides if necessary to flatten your fabric as much as possible. Cut away the ribbings if they are not going to be part of your garment. Cut the knits into squares or other chosen shapes. Use a rotary cutter and a straight edge, cutting on top of a self healing cutting mat for best results. This method will give you the smoothest and straightest edges.

Piecing the Fabric Cuts

In order to get a large enough piece of fabric for the pattern pieces of some garments, you may need to piece the felted wool into larger sections. Make a piece that is large enough to fit your pattern. Using your pattern piece as a guide, you can assemble a piece of fabric with the various pieces of felted sweaters positioned where you would like them to be on the finished garment.

1. Pin the cuts together, with edges overlapping, placing a piece of stabilizer under the seam area.

2. Machine stitch the pieces together. They can be stitched with a stitch of your choice — straight stitch, zig-zag, etc.

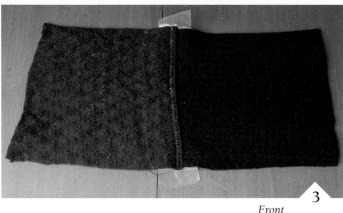

Front

Back

Cutting Out Pattern Pieces

1. Pin your pattern piece to your piece of "pieced" fabric.
2. Cut out the pattern using scissors.

If the pattern piece is small enough to be cut from one sweater or a part of a sweater, simply place the pattern on the felted fabric, pin the pattern to the fabric, and cut out the piece. Felted fabrics don't have grainlines so lining up the pattern on the "straight of the grain" is not a consideration.

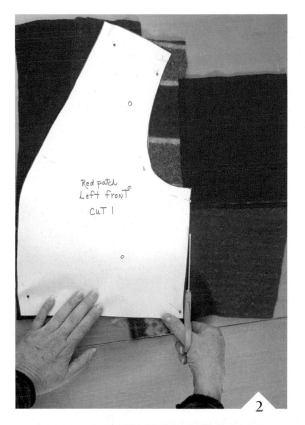

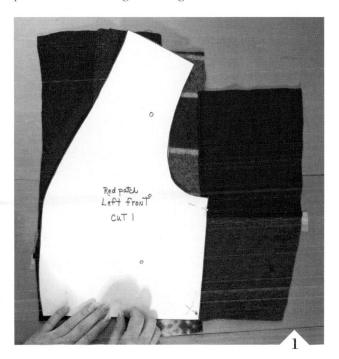

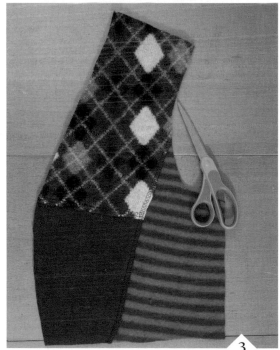

Sewing Felted Fabric

Joining Seams

There are two seaming options, standard seams and overlapped seams. For standard seams—the traditional method—place the fabric with right sides together, sew the seam, and turn to the right side. In this case, the seam is hidden. Or you can overlap the two seams and topstitch to join them.

On jackets, I often use a combination of the two options—I overlap the piecing and shoulder seams, but use the standard method for the side/underarm seam. (You can clip and trim the curve on the inside of the underarm seam for better fit.) I sew this seam last because then the overlaps are easy to reach.

On a vest, I often overlap all the seams. I like to use decorative machine stitches for sewing overlapped seams and for piecing felted fabrics, and I use a stabilizer sheet under all machine sewing to keep the seams from stretching out of shape as I sew.

Sewing Darts

If your pattern has darts, mark the dart and cut it out on the piece of felt. (Fig. 1) When sewing, overlap the edges of the cutout area, top over the bottom, gradually adjusting the overlap so the point of the dart blends into the jacket fabric and provides smooth shaping. Topstitch the overlap with a decorative machine stitch. (Fig. 2)

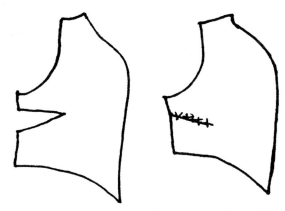

Fig. 1 - Cut out the dart.   Fig. 2 - Overlap and topstitch.

Adding a Tag to Your Project

When you've finished your felted creation, take a scrap of a felted sweater to use as a tag for your felted creation. Cut our the shape, use hand or machine embroidery to write your name or initials, and stitch in place.

Caring for Felted Wool Fashions

Caring for Felted Wool Fashions

You should care for your felted fashions as you would any fine washable. You can either wash items in cold water, using mild soap, then roll up in a clean towel to press out moisture, shape, and air dry flat **or** dry clean. During the summer, store your garments in moth proof bags. Wash or dry clean them before storing.

Making Flowers

*f*lowers made from felted sweaters make great brooches, belt buckles, and decorations for purses, slippers, jackets and hats. They are easy to make and don't require much fabric—a sweater sleeve or a few scraps are all you need. Embellish them with beads, embroidery, or yarn for extra pizzazz. Sew them in place or attach with a safety pin. This section includes instructions and patterns for making a variety of felted flowers.

Pictured clockwise from top left:
Round-on-Round Beaded Flower,
Tube Flower - Variation 1,
Tube Flower - Variation 3,
Tube Flower - Variation 2,
White Beaded Edge Rose,
Red Beaded Edge Rose,
Tube Flower - Variation 4.
Pictured at center:
Coiled Center Flower.

Tube Flowers

Tube flowers are made from sweater sleeves after they have been washed and dried. Here is the basic tube flower plus four variations. *The variations are pictured on page 35.*

SUPPLIES
- 6" from bottom of sweater sleeve plus ribbing
- Sewing needle
- Sewing thread

BASIC INSTRUCTIONS
1. Gather ribbed end 1" from edge and pull tight. This creates the center of the flower.
2. Turn under the other end and gather loosely, pulling just tight enough to make the raw edge roll under.

Tube Flower Variation 1
Cut a 2" length of sleeve tube. Gather 3/4" from one end to make flower center, pulling very tight. Secure thread. Turn up the remaining 1-1/4" so it cups around the center.

Tube Flower Variation 2
Cut a 3" length of sleeve tube. Gather to form the center 1" from the smaller end. Spread out the remaining 2" around the center.

Tube Flower Variation 3
Cut a 3" length of sweater tube. Gather 1" from the smaller end to form the center. Sew decorative yarn around the outside edge. ❋

Tube Flower Variation 4
I used a felted sleeve from a brown and white striped sweater to make this flower. I embellished it with lots of bright beads.

SUPPLIES
- 2" piece of a felted sweater sleeve or tube of felted wool
- 300 silver-lined rocaille beads
- 175 copper seed beads
- 100 opaque turquoise seed beads
- 50 translucent turquoise seed beads
- 50 iridescent purple seed beads
- 100 blue/purple iridescent bugle beads
- Sewing thread
- Beading needles
Optional:
- 3" dark felted wool circle (for backing)
- Heavy cardboard circle, 2-3/4" diameter
- Glue

INSTRUCTIONS
1. Sew rows of three silver-lined rocaille beads around the top of the tube, spacing the rows approximately 1/8" apart. (Fig. 1)
2. Sew running stitches to gather the top of the tube 1/2" from top edge to form the center of the flower. (The beads you sewed in step 1 will resemble the shape of flower petals. See the Bead Placement Chart.)
3. Sew three-bead rows of copper seed beads around the outside edge, spacing them 1/16" apart. See the Bead Placement Chart.
4. Use the Bead Placement Chart as a guide for sewing the remaining beads.
5. *Option:* To make a rigid flower, glue the cardboard circle to the back of the flower. Stitch the 4" felt circle over the back of the cardboard. ❋

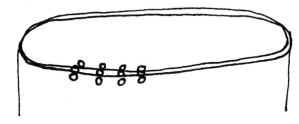

Fig. 1 - Sewing three-bead rows around the top of the tube.

Round-on-Round Beaded Flower

Tube Flower Variation 4
BEAD PLACEMENT CHART

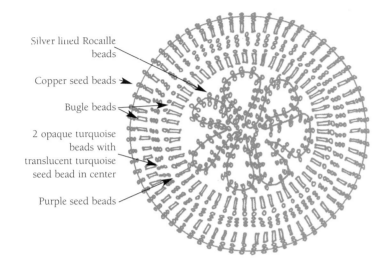

Silver lined Rocaille beads

Copper seed beads

Bugle beads

2 opaque turquoise beads with translucent turquoise seed bead in center

Purple seed beads

Round-on-Round Beaded Flower
BEAD PLACEMENT CHART

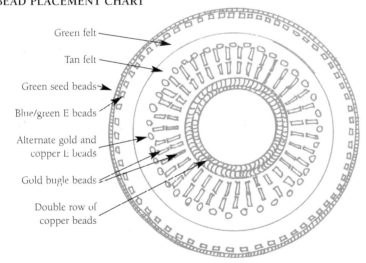

Green felt

Tan felt

Green seed beads

Blue/green E beads

Alternate gold and copper E beads

Gold bugle beads

Double row of copper beads

Round-on-Round
Beaded Flower
CENTER
EMBROIDERY CHART
Use this as a guide for color placement.

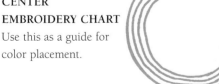

Brown

Tan

Orange

Variegated yellow/gold

SUPPLIES
- Green felted wool circle, 5" diameter
- Tan felted wool circle, 4" diameter
- 250 green metallic seed beads
- 210 copper brown seed beads
- 56 blue-green E-beads
- 12 copper E-beads
- 12 gold E-beads
- 50 gold bugle beads
- 6-strand embroidery floss - 1 skein variegated yellow/gold, 3 yds. brown, 3 yds. tan, 3 yds. orange
- Sewing thread to match felt circles
- Beading needles
- Tapestry needle

INSTRUCTIONS
Stitch the Beads;
See the Bead Placement Chart.
1. Thread green seed beads on thread.
2. Using a second needle and thread to match the felt, whipstitch the string of green beads along the edge of the green felt circle.
3. Sew blue-green E-beads 1/8" apart just inside the green seed bead circle.
4. Pin the tan circle to the center of the green circle.
5. String half the copper seed beads on thread. Whipstitch a circle of copper beads through both felt layers.
6. String the remaining copper seed beads. Use as many as needed to whipstitch a second row of copper seed beads inside the first one.

Embroider:
See the Center Embroidery Chart. As you stitch, the felt will stretch, causing the center to cup inward.
1. Inside the rows of copper beads, chain stitch a circle with brown floss and the tapestry needle.
2. Inside the brown circle, chain stitch a circle with tan floss.
3. Use variegated yellow/gold floss to chain stitch a spiral to the center of the flower. ❀

Coiled Center Flower

Two strips of felted wool, one with gray and black vertical stripes and one a solid light blue are rolled to form the center and placed on a petaled orange cutout.

SUPPLIES
- Striped strip of felted wool, 1" x 11"
- Solid strip of felted wool, 1" x 14"
- Solid felted wool, 5" square
- Sewing thread
- Sewing needle

INSTRUCTIONS
1. Tightly roll the striped wool strip to form a coil. Stitch to secure with a needle and thread.
2. Butt the end of the solid strip to the end of the striped strip and tightly roll the blue strip to continue the coil. Stitch to secure with needle and thread.
3. Using the pattern provided, cut out the petal piece from the felted square.
4. Sew the coiled center on top of the flower petal piece. ❀

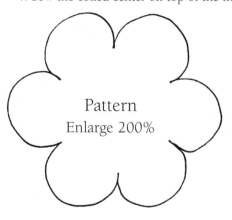

Pattern
Enlarge 200%

Beaded Edge Rose

SUPPLIES
- Felted wool (red, pink, coral, white, or other rose color)
- 600 (approx.) copper glass seed beads
- 1/2 yd. brass wire, 28 gauge
- Sewing thread to match wool
- Sewing needle
- Needlenose pliers

INSTRUCTIONS
1. Using the pattern provided, cut out the flower spiral.
2. Make a loop in one end of the wire that's large enough to keep the beads from falling off. Thread the beads on the wire.
3. Using a needle threaded with thread to match the wool, sew the loop end of the wire to the rose at A on Fig. 1.
4. Whipstitch the beaded wire along the edge of the spiral from point A to point B.
5. Twist the end of the wire into a tight coil. Trim the end.
6. Sew running stitches along the bottom edge of rose and pull tight to form the rose shape. Stitch to secure the thread. ❀

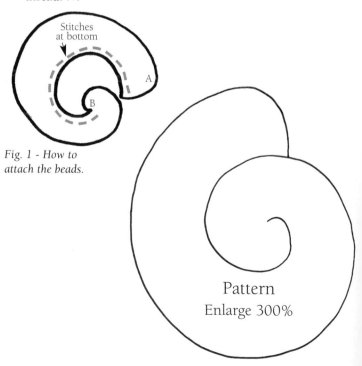

Stitches at bottom

Fig. 1 - How to attach the beads.

Pattern
Enlarge 300%

Felted Wool Projects

*h*ere they are! Capes and jackets and hats and tote bags and slippers and scarves and more. Felted fashions for women, for kids, for babies, for men—for everybody.

I've included a number of easy ideas for making purses and tote bags from felted sweaters, from casual carryalls to beaded beauties worthy of a night on the town. There are several options for purse closures. Flaps with buckles, especially heavy buckles, can be used to keep the purse closed, and magnetic closures can be added to any purse. Hook-and-loop dots or tape are ideal for lighter weight felted fabrics since they won't distort the shape of the bag—simply sew them on the purse.

Purse handles and straps are available at fabric and craft stores. You can also recycle handles from your old purses or from purses rescued from thrift shops. When I remove handles, I like to leave the connecting or attaching hardware, such as rings and hinges, attached to handles or straps by cutting them away from the purse below the hardware.

Each project includes a list of supplies you'll need and step-by-step instructions. You'll also find all the necessary patterns and numerous illustrations.

Capelet with Yarn Trim

This short cape uses several sweaters in similar tones of gray. A grid design was created with felted-look wooly yarn in a vibrant color and of a shape and size reminiscent of fettucine, the flat, ribbon-shaped noodle.

SUPPLIES
- Felted wool in grey tones
- Red felted-look ribbon style wool-and-acrylic yarn
- Black sewing thread
- Stabilizer
- Chalk
- Ruler
- Decorative button (as a closure)
- Flat gray button, 5/8" (to back the decorative button)
- Sewing needle

INSTRUCTIONS
1. Enlarge the patterns.
2. Using the pie-shaped section pattern, cut eight sections of felted wool.
3. Lay out the pieces, using the capelet shape pattern as a guide and overlapping the edges of the sections 1/4". Machine stitch along each overlapped edge. (Fig. 1)
4. Place the capelet shape pattern on top of the pieced sections. Cut out the cape. (Fig. 2)
5. To create the yarn grid in the lengthwise direction, start by covering the stitched overlaps between the sections. Place a second set of yarn pieces down the center of each section. (Fig. 3) Machine sew the yarn to the cape using a zig-zag stitch.
6. Use chalk and a ruler to mark the placement of the cross strips, making the marks 2-1/2" apart. See Fig. 4. Machine sew the yarn to the cape using a zig-zag stitch.
7. Try on the cape and mark the placement of the button and buttonhole. Sew the decorative button on the front and back it, on the inside, with the plain button. See "Buttonholes & Buttons" in the Basic techniques section.
8. Make a buttonhole. ✿

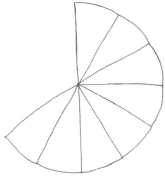

Fig. 1

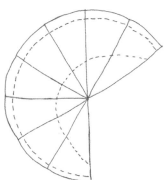

Fig. 2

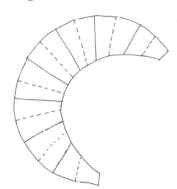

Fig. 3

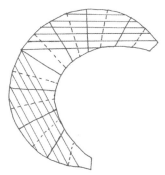

Fig. 4

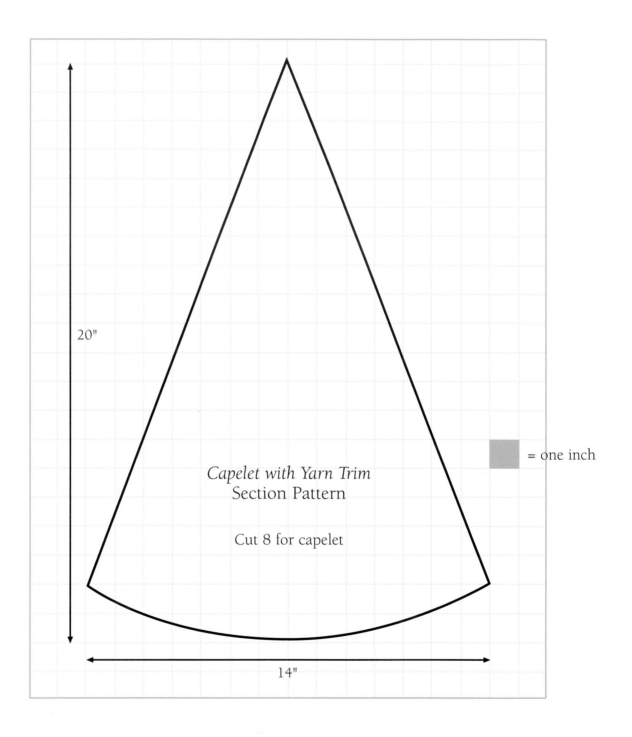

20"

Capelet with Yarn Trim
Section Pattern

Cut 8 for capelet

= one inch

14"

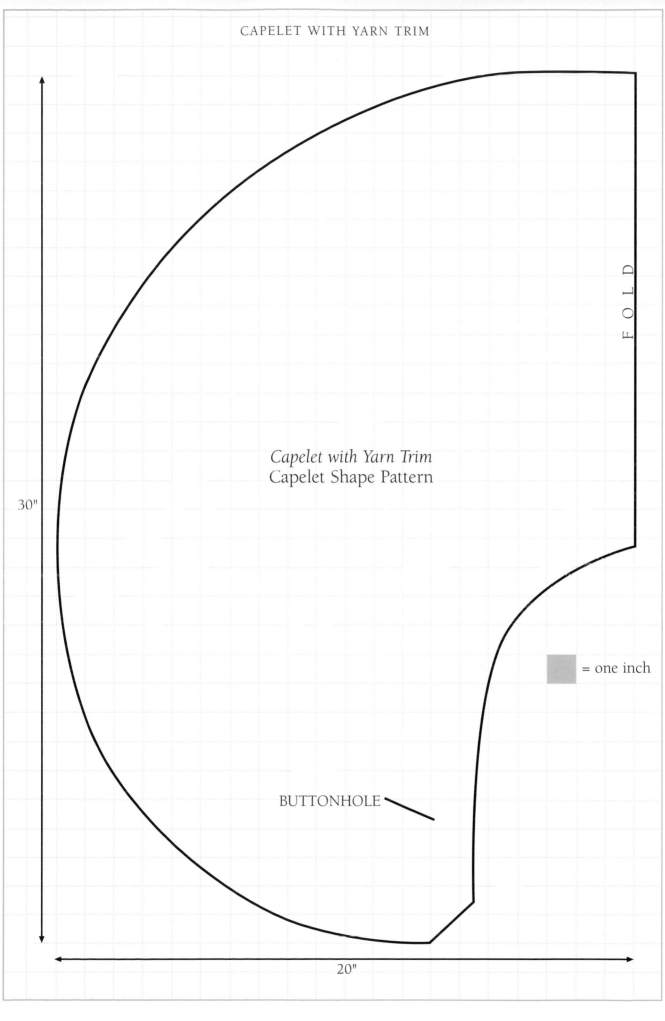

30"

F O L D

Capelet with Yarn Trim
Capelet Shape Pattern

= one inch

BUTTONHOLE

20"

Three-Button Vest

A rich combination of patterned felted sweaters are pieced to make this asymmetrical vest that closes with three decorative buttons.

SUPPLIES

- Felted wool pieces (enough to fit the pattern pieces)
- Dark sewing thread (or a color that blends with your fabric)
- 3 decorative buttons
- 3 plain buttons, 5/8", with the same number of holes as the decorative buttons

INSTRUCTIONS

1. Enlarge the pattern to the desired size.
2. Piece the felted wool to fit the pattern pieces.
3. Cut one back, one right front, and one left front from single thicknesses of pieced felted fabric.
4. Sew the darts with a decorative machine stitch. See "Sewing Darts" in the Making a Garment section.
5. Overlap the front shoulder seams over the back shoulder seams. Sew in place.
6. Overlap the side seams, front over back, and sew in place.
7. Make buttonholes on one front (right for women, left for men).
8. Add the buttons. (See "Buttonholes & Buttons" in the Basic Techniques section.) ✿

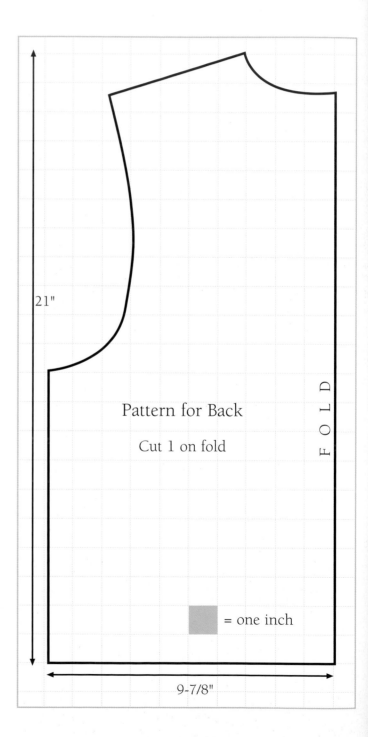

21"

Pattern for Back

Cut 1 on fold

FOLD

☐ = one inch

9-7/8"

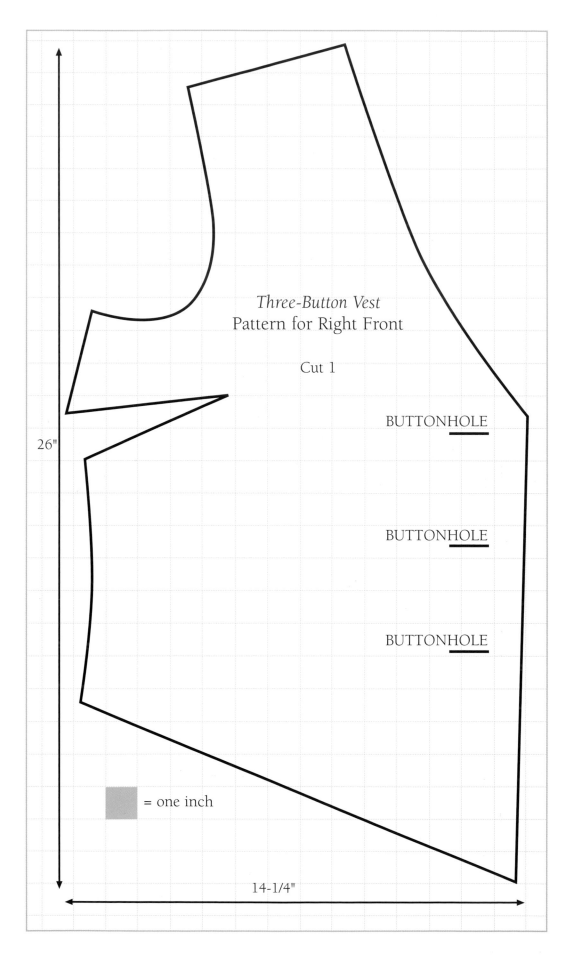

Three-Button Vest
Pattern for Right Front

Cut 1

BUTTONHOLE

BUTTONHOLE

BUTTONHOLE

26"

= one inch

14-1/4"

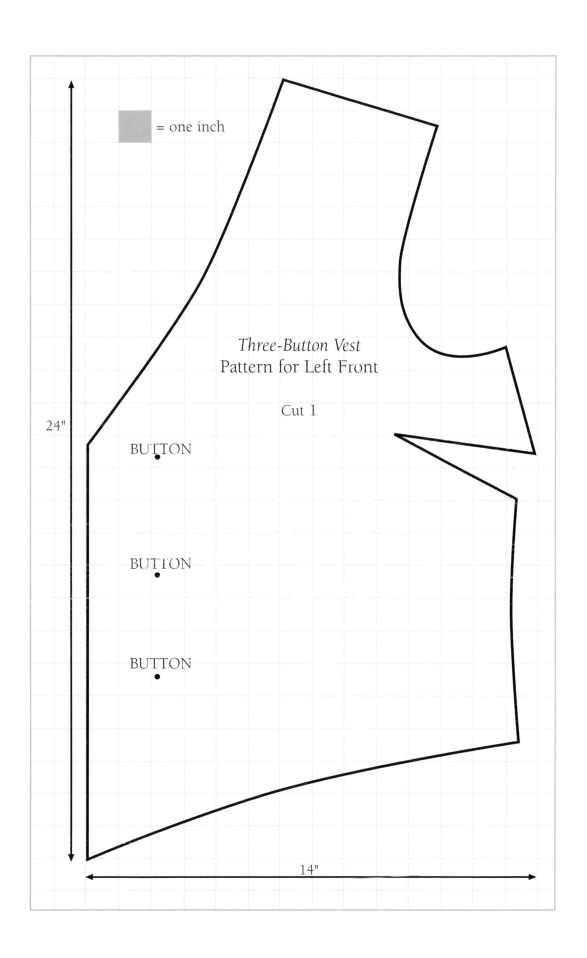

= one inch

Three-Button Vest
Pattern for Left Front

Cut 1

BUTTON

BUTTON

BUTTON

24"

14"

Wraparound Hipster Skirt

This simple wraparound skirt is made from felted wool sweater sleeves. I alternated patterned and solid pieces. Fitting is easy—simply take a body measurement where you want the top of the skirt to fit, then add or subtract sections to match the measurement plus the amount of overlap you want.

SUPPLIES
- Felted wool sleeves (one for each skirt section)
- Black grosgrain ribbon, 1-1/2" wide (measurement + overlap amount + 1")
- Dark sewing thread
- Stabilizer
- 6" black hook-and-loop fastener tape
- Large decorative safety pin

INSTRUCTIONS
1. Enlarge pattern as directed. Adjust pattern if you would like to make it shorter or longer. Use a measuring tape to measure the body where you want the top of the skirt. Use that measurement to determine how many pieces you'll need to cut.
2. Cut open the sleeves along the seam line and press flat.
3. Cut as many pattern pieces as needed, cutting one piece from each sleeve. You may need more or fewer, depending on the measurement.
4. Piece the skirt by overlapping the left sections over the right sections 1/4" and machine topstitch. Keep adding sections until you reach the number needed. (See Fig. 1.)
5. Pin the grosgrain ribbon to back side of the top edge. Turn under raw ends of ribbon at the ends. Topstitch along the top on the front with decorative machine stitches.
6. Sew the loop side of the hook-and-loop fastener to the ribbon on the underside of the overlap.
7. Cut the hook part of the hook-and-loop fastener 4". Sew to the underlapped part of the skirt on the top.
8. Sew the turned-under ends of the ribbon to the skirt.

To wear: Wrap the skirt around the body, and close with the hook-and-loop fastener. Secure with a decorative safety pin. (See Fig. 2.) ❀

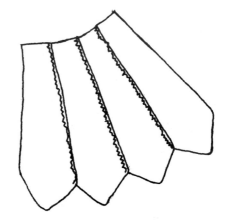

Fig. 1 - Piecing the sections.

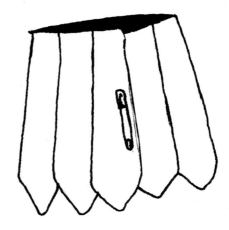

Fig. 2 - Placing the decorative safety pin.

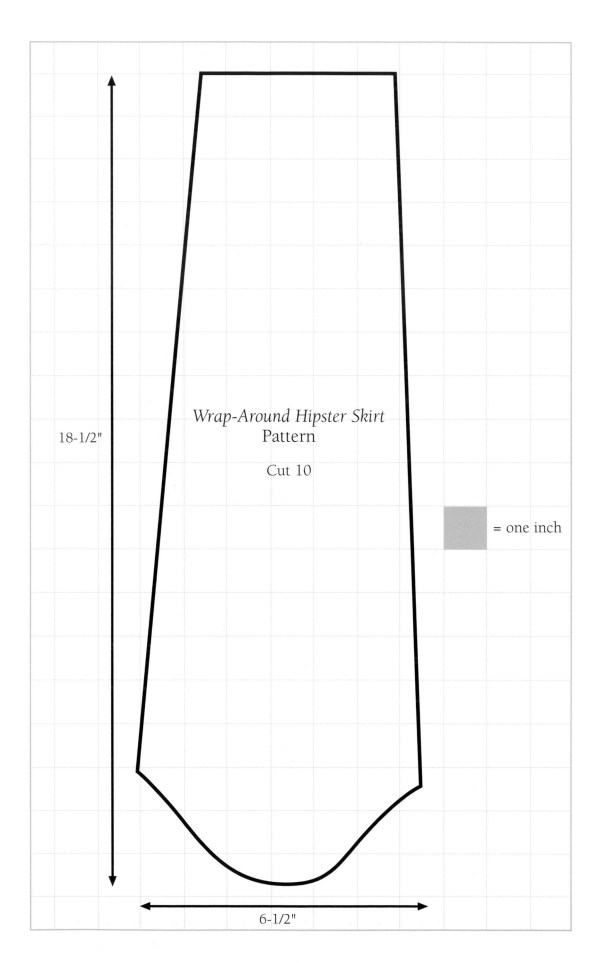

18-1/2"

Wrap-Around Hipster Skirt
Pattern

Cut 10

= one inch

6-1/2"

ADD-ON COLLAR
Instructions on page 52

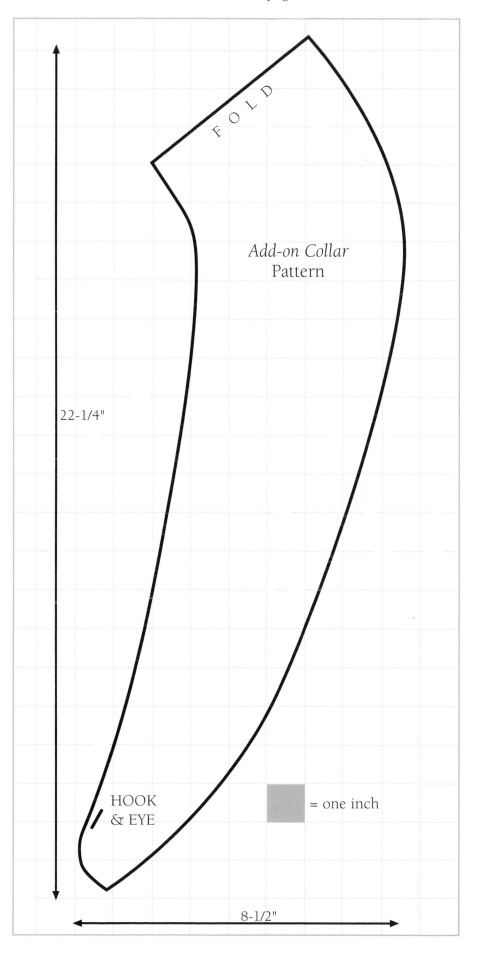

Add-on Collar
Pattern

F O L D

22-1/4"

HOOK
& EYE

= one inch

8-1/2"

Add-on Collar

This add-on collar is a snazzy detachable addition to a simple coat or jacket. You can make the felt fringe from sturdy or soft wool felt. I've given instructions for both options.

Pattern appears on page 51.

SUPPLIES
- Sturdy felted wool in dark color (for collar base)
- Soft or sturdy felted wool - Browns and blacks or colors of your choice (for the fur fringe)
- Black covered heavy duty large hook and eye
- Heavy duty black thread
- Sewing needle

INSTRUCTIONS
Make the Collar Base:
1. Enlarge the pattern piece.
2. Use the pattern piece to cut a collar base from sturdy felted wool.

Cut the Felt Fringe:
If you're using soft felt: Cut strips of felt 4" wide and 18" to 20" long. Fold each strip in half lengthwise and stitch 1/4" from the raw edges. (Fig. 1) Cut to fringe on the fold, making cuts 1-1/4" long and about 1/2" apart.

If you're using sturdy felt: Cut strips of felt 3" wide and 18" to 20" long. Cut fringe along one edge, making cuts 2" long and about 1/2" apart. (Fig. 2)

Attach the Fringe:
1. Sew a gathering stitch along the top (uncut) edge of each fringe strip. Pull the thread to gather each strip slightly.
2. Starting at the bottom ends of the collar, hand stitch the rows of fringe, overlapping them for a full look. (Most strips will make three rows.) Work both sides simultaneously so they are alike. See Fig. 3.
3. At the center back of the collar, add one last fringe strip where the two sides meet. Hand sew an overcast stitch between fringes to make the last strip stand up. (This last strip should cover any raw edges of the last two fringe strips.)
4. Sew the hook and eye at bottom of the collar on the inside. ✿

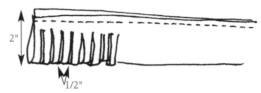
Fig. 1 - *Making fringe from soft felt.*

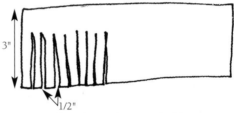
Fig. 2 - *Making fringe from sturdy felt.*

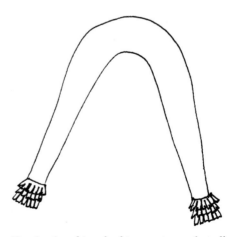
Fig. 3 - *Attaching the fringe strips to the collar base.*

Child's Easy Jumper Vest

This vest is so easy to make, fun to wear, and warm. Vary the colors, patterns, and buttons for a wealth of different looks.

SUPPLIES
• Light blue felted wool, 10" x 24"
• Medium blue felted wool (for straps)
• Striped felted wool in one, two, or four color combinations (for trim)
• 4 buttons, 7/8"
• 1 skein *each* of 5 different colors, 6-strand embroidery floss
• 2 yds. grosgrain ribbon, 1-1/2" wide
• Tapestry needle
• Sewing needle and blue thread (for sewing buttons)

INSTRUCTIONS
Cut:
1. Enlarge the pattern pieces.
2. Cut out the front and back from light blue.
3. Cut six medium blue strips, each 1-1/2" x 9".
4. Cut eight strips of striped wool, each 1-1/4" x 13" (two each of four types, four each of two types, or eight all alike).

Add Striped Trim:
1. Trim two striped strips to fit the top edge of the front and back pieces and pin in place. Using six strands of floss and the blanket stitch, attach the strips. (See "Hand Embroidery Stitches" in the Basic Techniques section.)
2. Trim two striped strips to fit the bottom edge of the front and back pieces and pin in place. Using six strands of floss and the blanket stitch, attach the strips.
3. Trim the striped strips to fit the sides of the front and back, letting the strips overlap the top and bottom strips at the corners. Using six strands of floss, blanket stitch them to the vest.

Add the Straps:
1. Cut two shoulder straps. Sew ribbon to the back of each to reinforce. Blanket stitch the sides of the straps.
2. Adjust the length of the straps to fit and sew them to the inside of the vest.
3. Cut four side straps. Cut four pieces of ribbon the same length of the strips plus 1". Sew the ribbon to the back of each strip to reinforce, folding under the ribbon ends. Blanket stitch around each strip.
4. Adjust the length to fit. Make a buttonhole in one end of each strip. See "Buttonholes & Buttons" in the Basic Techniques section.
5. Stitch the straps to the inside of the back of the vest.
6. Sew the buttons to the front of the vest to match the buttonholes. ✿

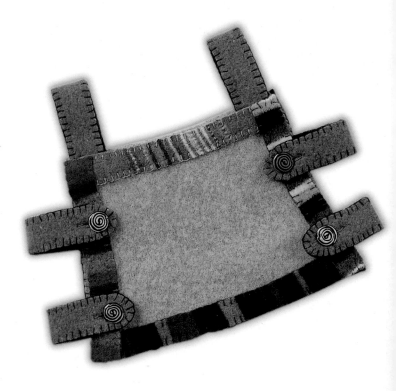

Child's Easy Jumper Vest
Patterns

Enlarge 145%

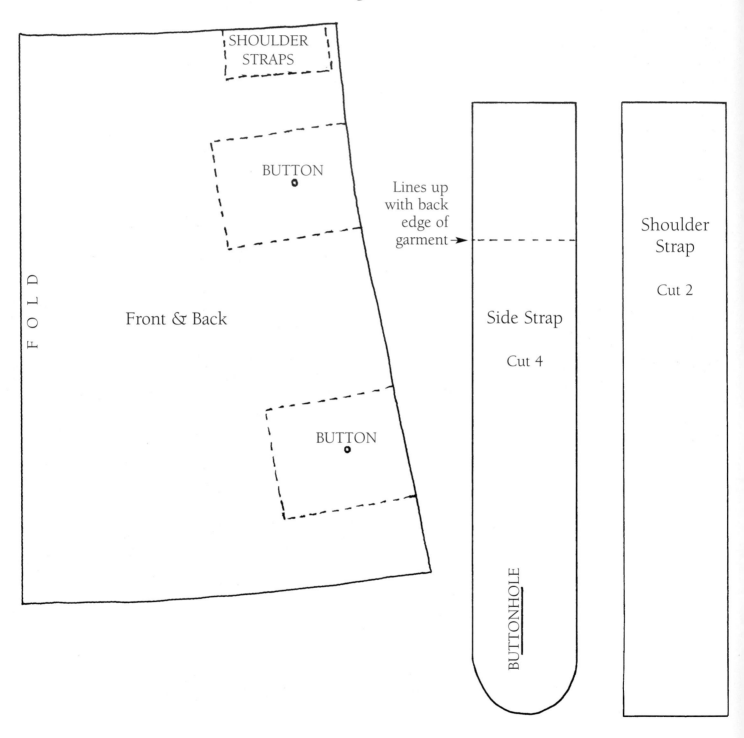

Simple Scarf

This really is simple! Choose a sweater with no noticeable difference between the ribbed trim and the body of the sweater.

SUPPLIES
• Felted wool man's sweater, size XXL large

INSTRUCTIONS
1. Cut a strip 7" wide from the bottom of the sweater. (Fig. 1)
2. Cut one side seam, leaving the other side seam intact. ❀

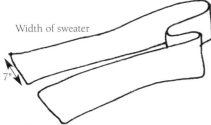

Width of sweater

7"

Fig. 1 - Cut a strip from the bottom of the sweater to make the scarf.

Doughnut Vest

This vest gets its name from the shape that the fabric is cut to make the vest. It is amazing how great it looks when it is slipped on. The doughnut shape makes an interesting backless vest with a large rounded collar. Choose a decorative button as a closure or add a special brooch.

SUPPLIES
- Felted wool in tones of gray
- Dark sewing thread and sewing needle
- Stabilizer
- Decorative button *or* brooch

INSTRUCTIONS
Make the Pattern:
See Fig. 1. You can use the sizes listed as a guide if you can't measure the body.

1. Measure the distance across the back, from underarm to underarm. (This measurement is the diameter of the inner (cutout) circle in Fig. 1.) Draw a circle whose diameter is this measurement.
2. For the diameter of the outer circle, add 18" to the diameter of the inner circle. Draw the outer circle.
3. Cut out the doughnut-shaped pattern (Fig. 1). Divide the pattern in fourths and cut apart. Use the four parts to construct vest.

Construct the Vest:

1. Assemble four pieces of felted wool, one for each pattern piece, adding 1/4" to the sides of each piece for seam allowances.
2. Overlap the seam allowances and sew the pieces together with a decorative machine stitch.
3. Try on the vest and adjust for best fit. Mark the placement of the button and buttonhole.
4. Make a buttonhole on the right and sew the button on the left side. See "Buttonholes & Buttons" in the Basic Techniques section. *Option:* Use a brooch instead of a button to close the vest. ❁

Variations: Divide the pattern into smaller pieces. Vary the colors.

Size Guide

	FROM UNDERARM TO UNDERARM	ACROSS THE BACK
Small	10"	28"
Medium	13"	31"
Large	16"	34"
Extra Large	18"	36"

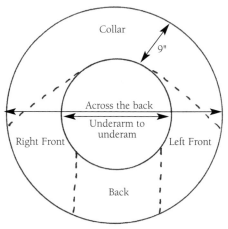

Fig. 1 - Pattern

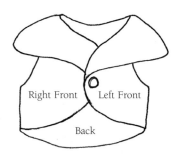

Pieced Shrug

This shrug can be worn several ways—with the front ends loose, with one front end flipped over the opposite shoulder, with both front ends flipped over the opposite shoulders, or with the front ends tied in a flip-over knot in front.

SUPPLIES
• 6 (approx.) felted wool sweaters
• Sewing thread

INSTRUCTIONS
1. Enlarge the patterns.
2. Piece together felted wool to fit the patterns, using angled pieces as shown in Fig. 1.
3. Place the pattern on top of the pieced fabric and cut out. See Fig. 2 for an example.
4. Sew the shoulder seams by overlapping the fronts of the shrug over the back at the shoulder and top stitching.
5. Sew the sleeve and side seams by folding the fabric with right sides together. Use a 1/2" seam allowance. Trim the seam and turn to the right side.
6. Topstitch along the back neck edge to prevent stretching. ❀

Fig. 1 - Piecing layout for the front pieces. Use the same piecing style for the back.

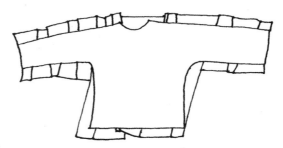

Fig. 2 - The back pattern positioned on the felted, pieced wool.

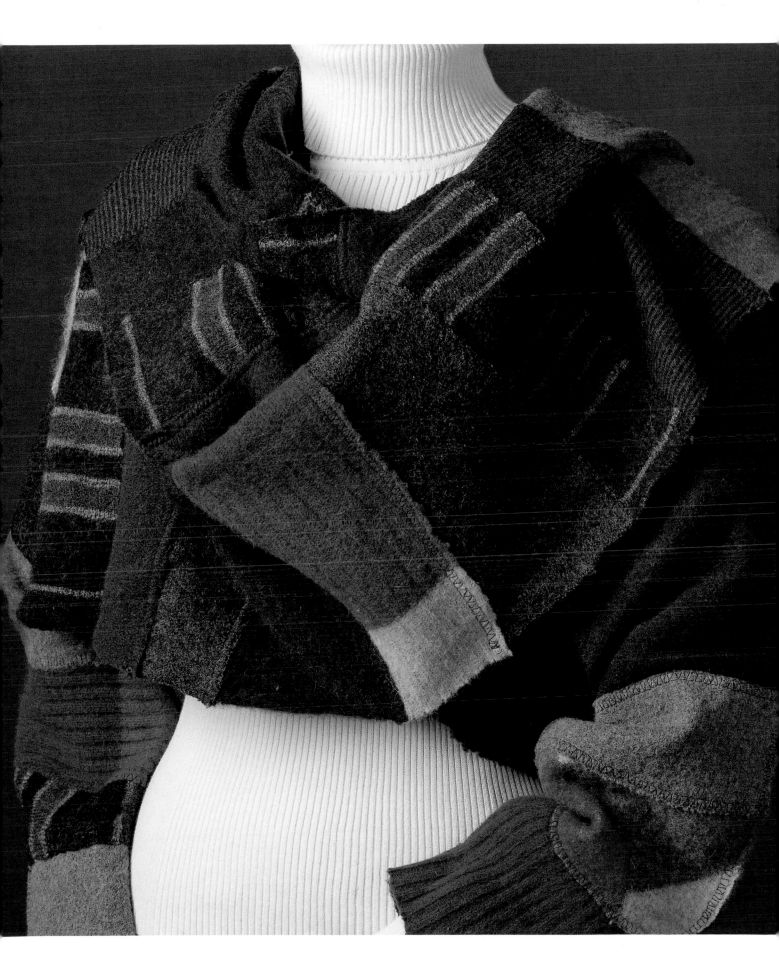

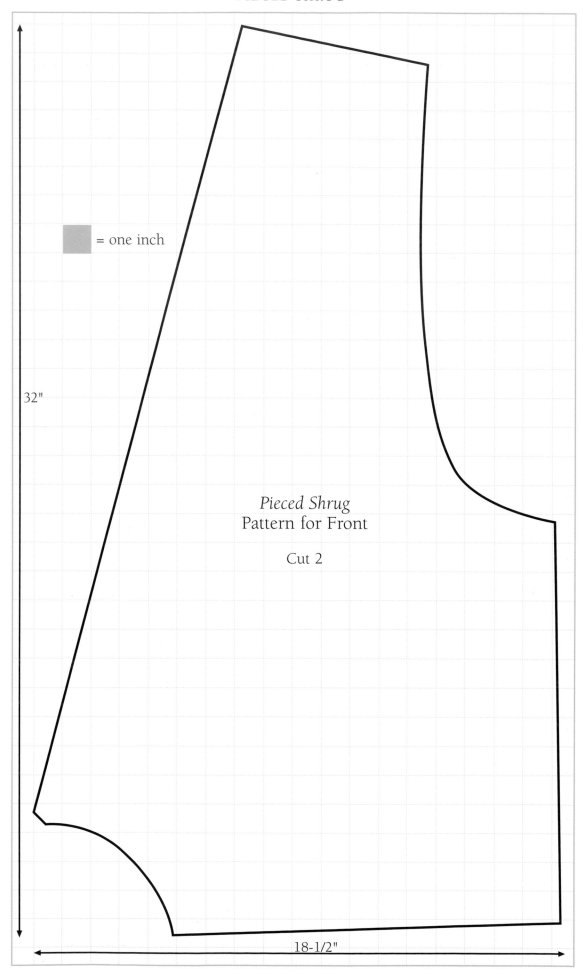

= one inch

32"

Pieced Shrug
Pattern for Front

Cut 2

18-1/2"

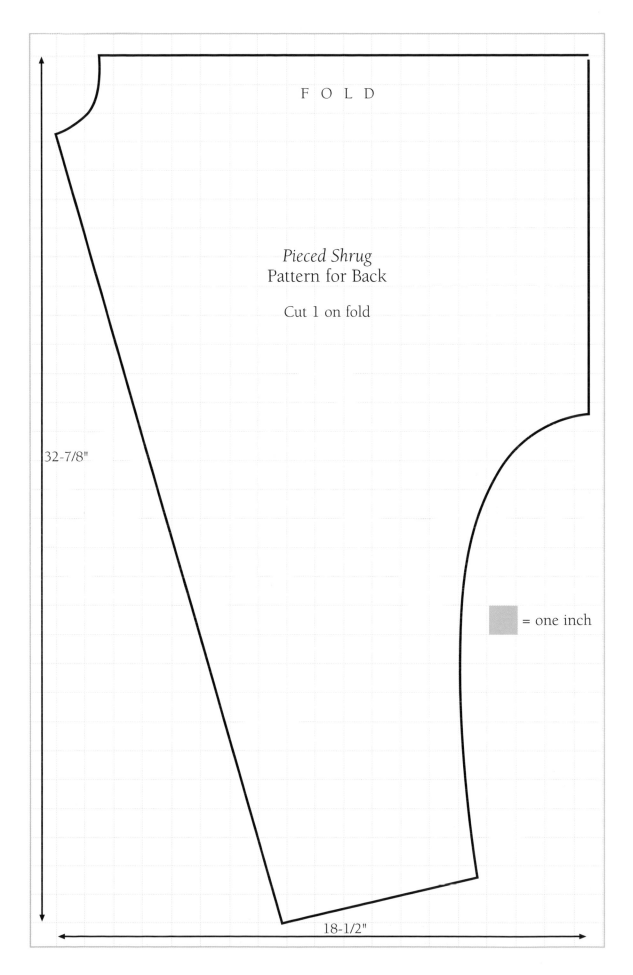

FOLD

Pieced Shrug
Pattern for Back

Cut 1 on fold

32-7/8"

= one inch

18-1/2"

Ribbon Edge Jacket

A mix of solid and patterned sweaters are combined to make this simple jacket. Ribbon yarn is handstitched to all the edges to bring everything together.

SUPPLIES
- Felted wool, pieced to fit pattern pieces
- Ribbon yarn
- Large eye needle, tapestry or darning
- Dark sewing thread

INSTRUCTIONS
1. Enlarge patterns.
2. Cut out two fronts and one back.
3. With right sides together and using a sewing machine, sew shoulder seams and underarm seams, using a 5/8" seam allowance.
4. Turn to right side.
5. Using an overcast stitch and ribbon yarn, trim all the outside edges, including the sleeve ends. ❀

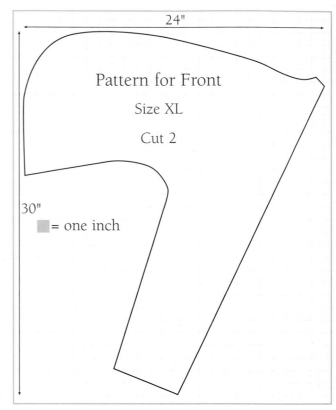

24"

Pattern for Front

Size XL

Cut 2

30"

■ = one inch

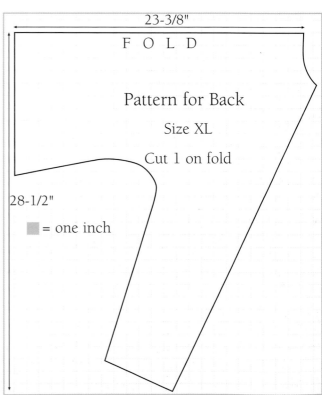

23-3/8"

F O L D

Pattern for Back

Size XL

Cut 1 on fold

28-1/2"

■ = one inch

Executive Shawl

I used scrap pieces of felted wool to make this shawl, including pieces of patterned knits and appliqued knits.

SUPPLIES
- Scrap pieces of felted wool
- Black sewing thread
- Heavy duty water-soluble stabilizer
- Button
- Sewing needle

INSTRUCTIONS
See Fig. 1.

1. Piece the scraps of felted wool in various widths by overlapping them 3/8" to form strips 21" long.
2. Place stabilizer under the overlapped areas and use a zig-zag stitch (or any wide stitch) to join the pieces.
3. Join these strips by overlapping them 3/8" and stitching them together, side by side, to form a shawl 21" wide and 54" long.
4. Try on the shawl to determine the placement of the button and buttonhole. Mark the placement of the button and buttonhole.
5. Attach the button. Make a buttonhole to fit. See "Buttonholes & Buttons" in the Basic Techniques section. ✿

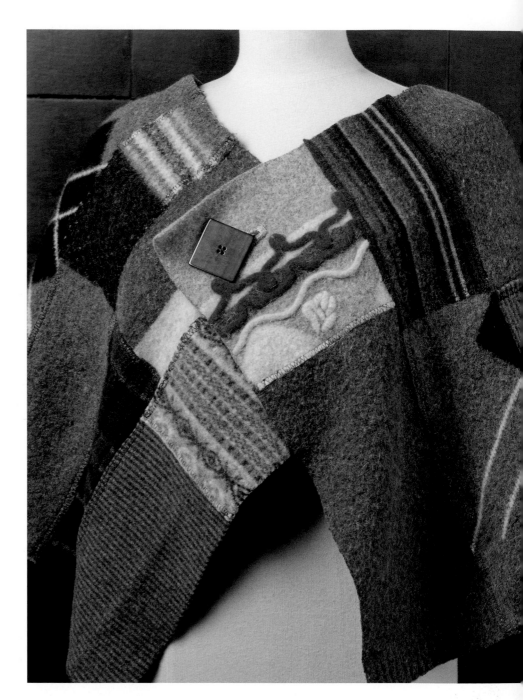

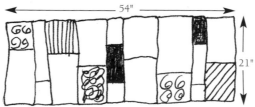

Fig. 1 - Piecing diagram

Flouncy Scarf

This scarf uses the felted ribbing from the bottoms of four sweaters as decoration for the ends.

SUPPLIES

- Felted wool (enough to make the scarf)
- 4 felted wool sweaters with ribbed bottoms
- Dark sewing thread
- Stabilizer
- Sewing thread to match each ribbing section

INSTRUCTIONS

1. Piece together a scarf that measures 7-1/2" wide and 68" long.
2. Cut the ribbing off the bottoms of the four sweaters.
3. Cut the ribbing into pieces that will wrap around the ends of the scarf plus a 1/2" seam allowance (16" approximately).
4. Sew 1/2" seams to join the ends of each ribbing piece to make a tube.
5. Using thread to match the ribbing, sew one ribbing tube on each end of the scarf, 1" up from the bottom. See Fig. 1.
6. Sew a second ribbing tube above the first one so the bottom of the second one slightly covers the top of the first. See Fig. 2. ❀

Fig. 1 - The scarf with one ribbing tube sewed to each end.

Fig. 2 - The scarf with two ribbing tubes sewed to each end.

Flower Cape

This simple cape in shades of gray is adorned with a bright red felted wool flower.

SUPPLIES
- Felted wool - Grays and blacks, scraps of red
- Sewing thread - Black, red
- Large black covered hook and eye
- Stabilizer
- Sewing needle

INSTRUCTIONS

Make the Cape:
1. Enlarge the pattern pieces.
2. Piece gray and black felted wool to fit the three pattern pieces. Cut out.
3. Sew the pieces together, overlapping them and machine stitching with a decorative stitch. See Fig. 1.
4. From gray felted wool, cut a strip 32" long and 2" wide.
5. Pin one long side of the strip over the top 1/4" of the cape on the right side. Machine stitch to the cape neckline with a decorative stitch. See Fig. 2.
6. Fold the strip in half lengthwise. Sew the second long side to the inside of the cape, forming the neckband. Sew the ends closed.

Make the Flower:
1. Using the patterns provided, cut a large flower from red felted wool and a smaller flower from black felted wool.
2. Cut a 2" x 6" strip of red felt.
3. Fringe one long side of the red felted strip by making cuts 1-3/4" long and 1/4" apart.
4. To make the flower center, roll the strip into a tight coil and stitch to secure, using a needle and red thread.
5. Pin the black flower piece on top of the red flower piece. Sew a gathering stitch in a 1" circle through both flowers. (Fig. 3) Pull the threads tight to pucker the flower.
6. Sew the base of the coiled fringe flower center over the gathered circle.

Assemble:
1. Sew the flower to top left side of the cape.
2. Sew the hook side of the hook and eye inside the cape under the flower.
3. Sew the eye of the hook and eye 2" from right end of the neckband. ❈

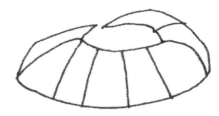

Fig. 1 - The pieces of the cape.

Fig. 2 - Adding the strip to make the neckband.

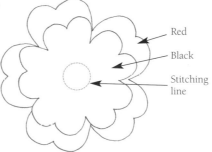

Red

Black

Stitching
line

Fig. 3 - Flower assembly diagram.

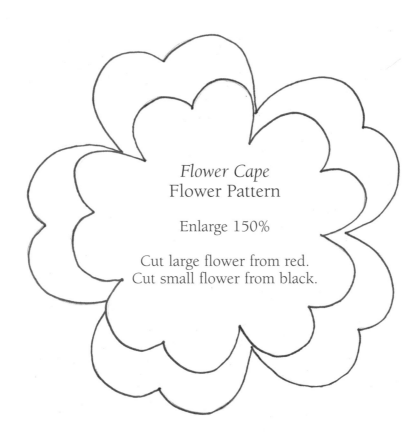

Flower Cape
Flower Pattern

Enlarge 150%

Cut large flower from red.
Cut small flower from black.

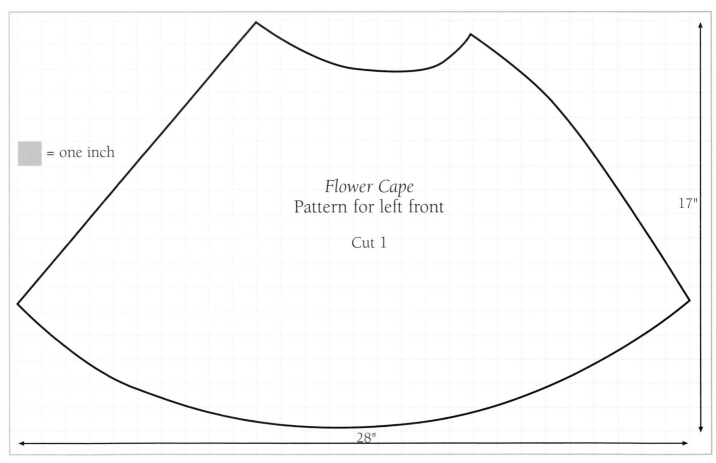

= one inch

Flower Cape
Pattern for left front

Cut 1

17"

28"

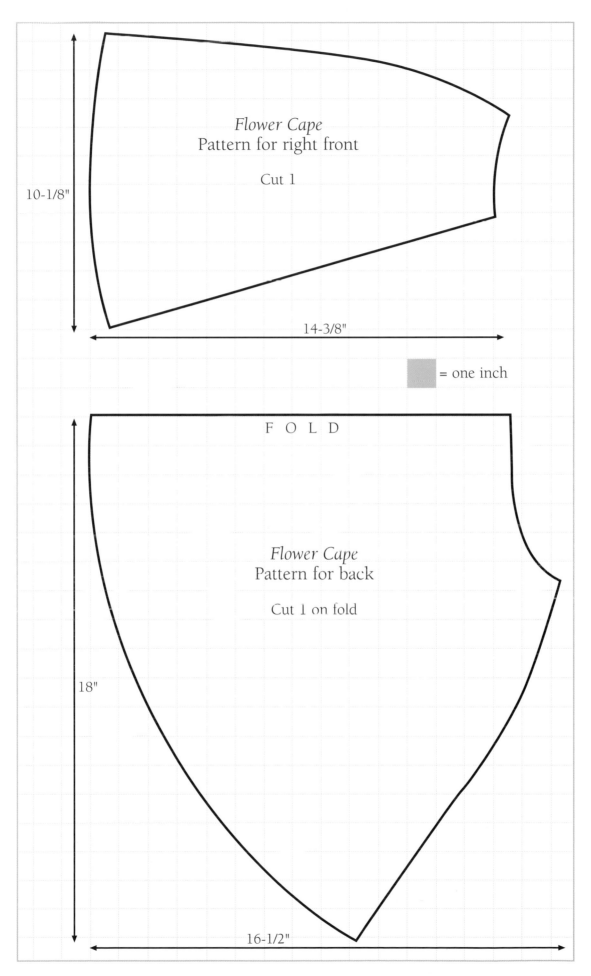

Flower Cape
Pattern for right front

Cut 1

10-1/8"

14-3/8"

= one inch

F O L D

Flower Cape
Pattern for back

Cut 1 on fold

18"

16-1/2"

Multicolored Woven Scarf

This fun scarf is constructed from felted-look wooly yarn that is the shape and size of fettucine, the flat, ribbon-shaped noodle and scraps of felted wool. You'll need a flat surface at least six feet long for weaving the scarf.

SUPPLIES
- Felted-look ribbon style wool-and-acrylic knitting yarn - multicolor with bright pink, orange, and fuchsia
- Large eye needle, darning or tapestry
- Assorted colors of wool yarn *or* 6-strand embroidery floss
- Assorted materials for weaving - Felted wool, yarns, floss, decorative trims
- Tape, masking

INSTRUCTIONS
1. Cut felted-look ribbon-style yarn into five lengths, each 2 yds. long.
2. Place the five yarn pieces on a flat surface long enough to accommodate the length of the scarf, leaving 1/4" between them.
3. Secure the yarn pieces to your work surface with tape at both ends, placing the tape 6" from the ends. (These free ends will become the fringe.) See Fig. 1.
4. Cut narrow strips of felted wool (5/8" x 5-1/2") for weaving.
5. Weave strips over and under the yarn pieces. Alternate wool strips and short pieces of felted-look yarn, leaving space between them for various decorative trims.
6. Secure the wool strips and felted-look yarn pieces by sewing a knot at each cross over or color of wool using wool yarn or embroidery floss. See Fig. 2.
7. Between the wool strips and yarn pieces, wrap yarns and trims around the yarn lengths. Trim ends to 1/2". See Fig. 3.
8. When you have finished weaving the scarf, remove the tape. ❋

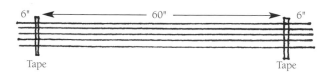

Fig. 1 - Layout for yarn.

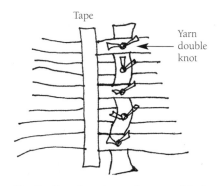

Fig. 2 - Securing pieces of yarn or felted strips with knots.

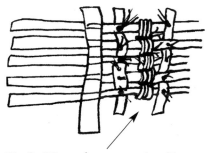

Fig. 3 - Wrapped yarns are placed between strips of felted wool and felted-look yarn pieces. The ends are tied together and trimmed.

Woven Strip Gray Scarf

This woven scarf is made entirely from felted wool strips. You'll need a flat surface at least six feet long for a work surface.

SUPPLIES
- Assorted gray felted wool sweaters
- Large eye needle, tapestry or darning
- 30 yds. black pearl cotton #5 thread *or* 3-ply black wool yarn
- Tape, masking

INSTRUCTIONS

1. Cut five strips of felted wool from the sweaters, 5/8" wide and 2 yds. long. See "Cutting Long Strips" in the Basic Techniques section.
2. Place the five strips on your work surface to form the base (warp) of the scarf, leaving about 1/4" between each strip. (Fig. 1)
3. With tape, secure the strips to your work surface at both ends, placing tape 6" from the ends. (These free ends will become the fringe.) See Fig. 1.
4. Cut approximately 55 shorter strips, 5/8" wide and 5-1/2" long.
5. Weave these shorter strips through the base strips, leaving 1/4" between them. See Fig. 2. Keep adding strips every 1/4" until you reach the second piece of tape.
6. Using a needle and yarn, secure the shorter strips to the base strips where they intersect, stitching from the top through both strips and coming back up through both strips. Tie the yarn in a double knot, tighten, and trim the ends of the yarn 1/2" from the knot. Repeat at every intersection to secure all the strips. (Fig. 3)
7. Remove the tape. ❀

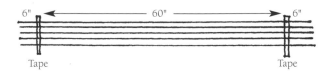

Fig. 1 - Layout for yarn.

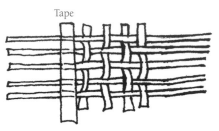

Fig. 2 - Weaving the shorter strips through the long warp strips.

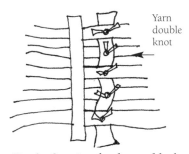

Fig. 3 - Securing the shorter felted strips with yarn knots.

Cozy Slippers

Suitable for men, women, or children, these simple slippers have layered soles and non-skid fabric bottoms.

SUPPLIES
- Two colors of felted wool
- Heavyweight double-sided stiff fusible interfacing, 10" x 12"
- Non-skid slipper fabric, 10" x 12"
- #5 pearl cotton thread (Choose a color to accent the felt.)
- Sewing thread to match top layer of slipper
- Tearaway stabilizer
- Quilting needle
- Tapestry needle

INSTRUCTIONS
Cut:
1. Enlarge the patterns to fit the size of the foot for which you are making them.
2. Cut out two slipper tops and two slipper top linings. Be sure to turn the pattern over to make left and right versions of each piece.
3. Cut two soles (left and right versions) in two colors of felted wool.
4. Cut two soles (left and right versions) from non-skid fabric.
5. Cut two soles (left and right versions) from fusible interfacing. Trim 3/8" from these pieces all around so they are smaller than the pattern.

Assemble:
1. Sandwich the fusible interfacing between the two felt layers of the sole of one slipper. Following the interfacing manufacturer's instructions, fuse the layers together. Repeat for the other slipper.
2. Place the non-skid fabric, bumpy side down, on top of the tearaway stabilizer. Pin the felt "sandwich" on top. Machine stitch both slippers all around 1/3" from the edge. Remove the tearaway stabilizer.
3. Place slipper top on the slipper top lining. Bend the pieces into shape to accommodate the foot. Trim the lining piece as needed. Pin the top of the slipper to the sole. Repeat for the other slipper.
4. Using matching thread and a quilting needle, baste all the layers together, stitching about 1/4" from the edges. Repeat for the other slipper.
5. Using pearl cotton thread and a tapestry needle, blanket stitch all around the sole, attaching the slipper top to the sole. Repeat to complete the other slipper. ❄

Cut patterns as follows:

Slipper Top - Left foot
- Turn over to cut right foot.
- Cut one for each foot for top
- Cut one for each foot for top lining

Slipper Sole - Left foot
- Turn over to cut right foot.
- Cut 1 for each foot from same fabric as slipper top
- Cut 1 for each foot from lining
- Cut 1 for each foot from fusible interfacing
- Cut 1 for each foot from non-skid fabric

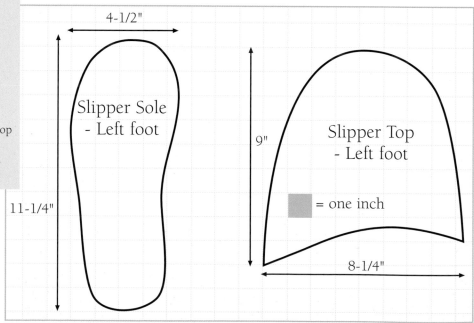

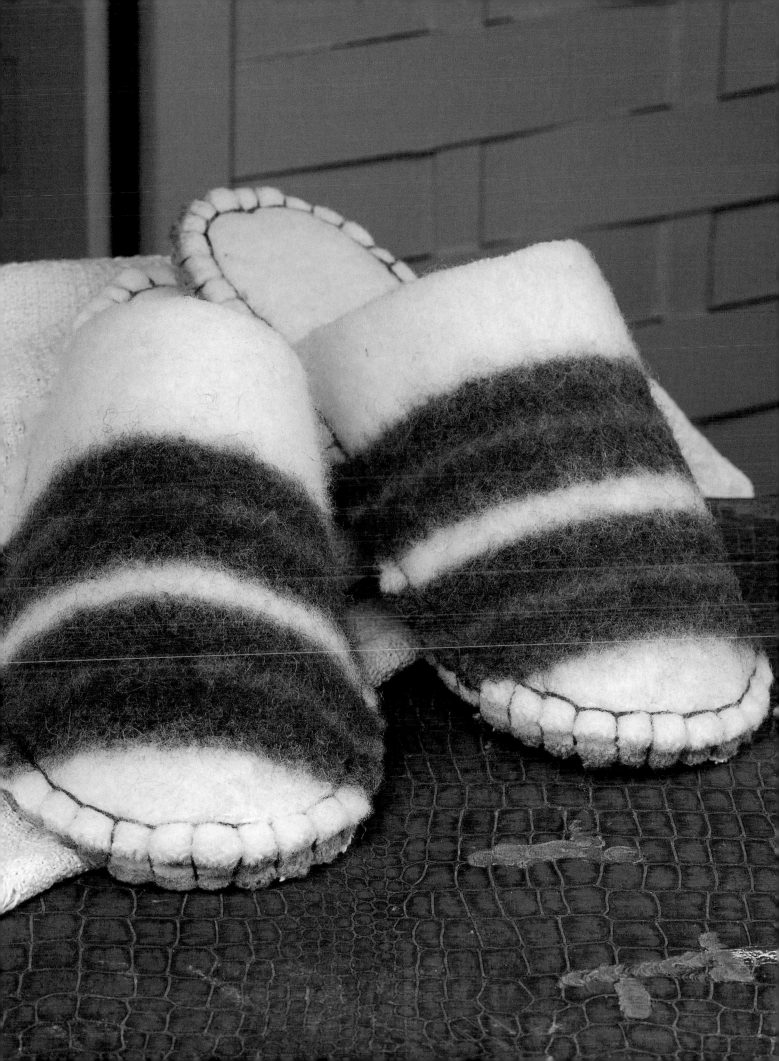

Flowered Slippers

These warm and wooly slippers are shown with sparkling beaded flowers, though they'd be just as cozy without them. The slippers have non-skid fabric bottoms and elasticized backs for a snug, comfortable fit.

SUPPLIES
- Felted wool
- Stabilizer
- Heavyweight double-sided fusible interfacing, 10" x 12"
- Non-skid fabric, 10" x 12"
- Black #5 pearl cotton thread (or color to accent felt)
- Sewing thread (to match wool)
- 1/4 yd. elastic, 1/4" wide
- Tapestry needle

INSTRUCTIONS

Cut the Soles:
1. Enlarge patterns to fit.
2. Cut four soles from felted wool.
3. Cut two soles from fusible interfacing. Trim 3/8" from all edges.
4. Cut two soles from non-skid fabric.

Assemble the Soles:
1. Stack the pieces for each foot in this order: felted wool, fusible interfacing, felted wool, and non-skid fabric. (Fig. 1) Sew basting stitches down the center of the stack.
2. Place stabilizer on the bottom of the stack. Machine stitch around outsides of each set of the soles 1/4" from the edges.

Cut & Assemble the Tops:
1. Cut two shoe backs. Cut two pieces of elastic, each 4-1/2".
2. On the wrong side of shoe back, just below the fold line, sew a piece of elastic, stretching the elastic to fit. (Fig. 2)
3. Cut four shoe tops. Stack two together and, with stabilizer on the bottom, sew each set together along the U-shaped (inner) edge. (Fig. 3)
4. Fold each shoe back in half with the elastic on the inside. Pin one back to one top, allowing the ends of the backs to cover the ends of the front by 1/4". With matching thread, sew together by stitching over the edge of the shoe back. (Fig. 4)
5. Pin one shoe top to one shoe bottom. Sew together with a blanket stitch, using pearl cotton and tapestry needle. See the Techniques section for instructions on blanket stitching. (Fig. 5)

Wool
Interfacing
Wool
Non-skid fabric
Bottom of sole

Fig. 1 - How to stack the pieces for the soles.

Fig. 2 - How to sew the elastic on the shoe back.

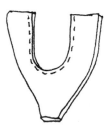

Fig. 3 - Stitching the layered shoe tops.

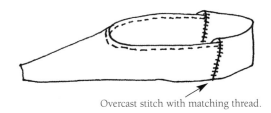

Overcast stitch with matching thread.

Fig. 4 - Sewing the back to the top.

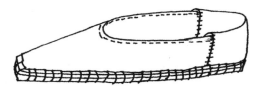

Fig. 5 - Sewing the tops to the soles.

Beaded Flowers for Slippers

I used a felted sweater sleeve with three stripes of different colors to make these flowers, which I decorated with bronze and black seed beads. The stripes on my sweater were 1/2" wide.

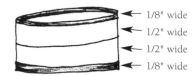

Fig. 1 - Cutting Diagram

SUPPLIES

- 1 felted wool sweater sleeve
- Black sewing thread
- 1800 (approx.) bronze seed beads
- 200 (approx.) black seed beads
- Sewing needle
- Beading needle

Fig. 2 - Gathering one end of the tube forms the flower shape.

INSTRUCTIONS

Cut & Sew:

1. Leave the sleeve round—**don't** cut along the seam. Cut two identical tube-shaped pieces 2-1/4" wide. I used 1/8" of the first stripe, a whole stripe (1/2"), another whole stripe (1/2"), and 1/8" of the last stripe. See Fig. 1.

2. Sew stitches to gather each tube just below the 1/8" wide stripe. Pull thread very tight. (This forms the flower shape.) See Fig. 2.

Fig. 3 - Beading Diagram

Add Beads:

See Fig. 3.

1. Add three bronze seed beads every 1/8" all around the outside of the flower on the 1/8" wide stripe.

2. Sew lines of bronze seed beads around the inner 1/2" wide stripe. Space the lines about 1/8" apart and use six to nine beads on each one.

3. Sew black seed beads randomly on the gathered center section. ❀

Flowered Slippers
Pattern for Back

Enlarge 150%

Cut 2 from felted wool

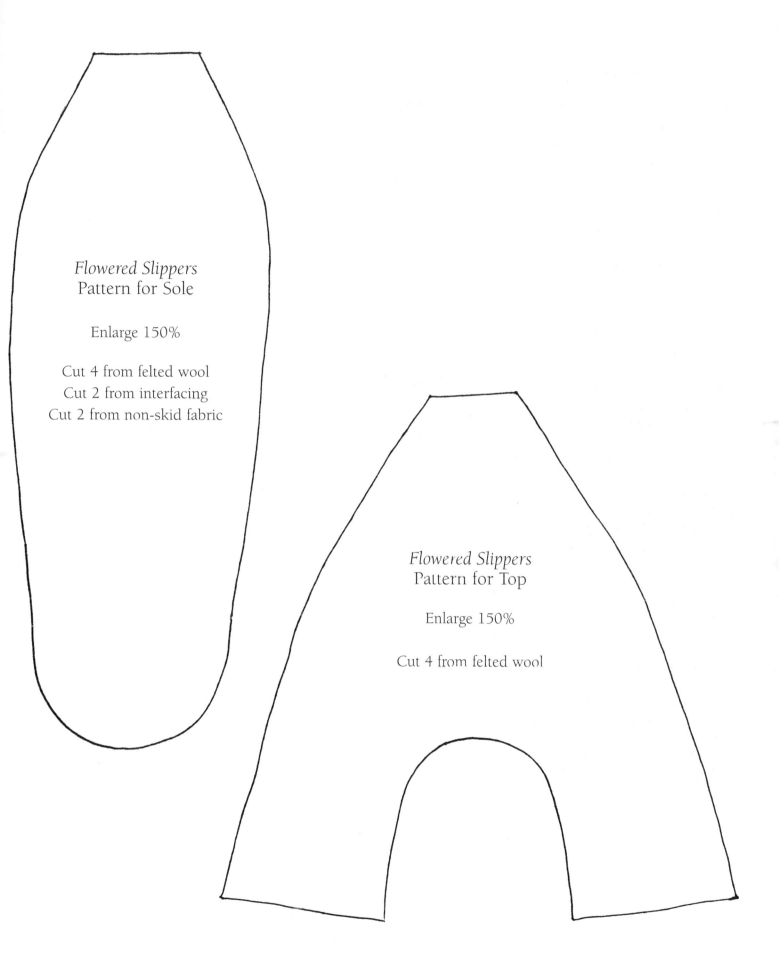

Flowered Slippers
Pattern for Sole

Enlarge 150%

Cut 4 from felted wool
Cut 2 from interfacing
Cut 2 from non-skid fabric

Flowered Slippers
Pattern for Top

Enlarge 150%

Cut 4 from felted wool

Tassel Hat & Mitten Scarf

I used a blue striped sweater to make this hat and scarf set. The mittens are attached to the ends of the scarf so you'll never lose them. Blanket stitching with black wool yarn is used to edge both pieces.

Tassel Hat

SUPPLIES
- Blue striped felted wool
- 3-strand wool yarn - Navy blue
- Large eye needle, tapestry or darning
- Sewing thread - blue
- Sewing needle

INSTRUCTIONS
1. Enlarge hat pattern.
2. Cut out front and back of hat.
3. To make the tassel, cut 15 strips across the stripes of the sweater, each 1/2" wide and 8" long. Hold each strip by the ends and tug gently to stretch.
4. Run a threaded needle through one end of each strip and bring the strips together on the thread. Wrapping them together like a tassel, secure with thread.
5. With wrong sides together and the gathered end of the tassel inserted at the top of the hat, baste the front and back together, leaving the bottom (flat side) open.
6. Using three strands of yarn, blanket stitch around the sides and top of the hat. See the Techniques sections for blanket stitching instructions.
7. *Option:* Turn up the bottom of the hat to make a cuff. ❈

Mitten Scarf

SUPPLIES
- Felted wool in tones of blue
- Navy blue 3 strand wool yarn
- Sewing thread - Blue
- Stabilizer
- Large eye needle, tapestry or darning

INSTRUCTIONS
1. Enlarge mitten pattern as needed.
2. Cut 1 mitten from felted wool. Turn over pattern and cut a second mitten. Set aside.
3. Use the mitten pattern and Fig. 1 to cut out a scarf as wide as the straight wrist edge of the mitten. It should measure 79" long from mitten finger end to mitten finger end.
4. With right sides out, place the mitten you set aside in step 2 on top of the ones on the ends of the scarf. (Fig. 2) Sew around the mittens 1/4" from edge, using stabilizer under the machine stitching. Trim away any uneven edges.
5. Blanket stitch around entire edge of scarf and mittens with three strands of yarn. See the Techniques section for stitching instructions. ❈

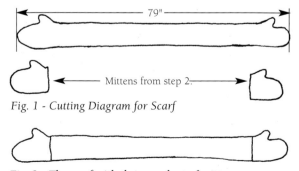

79"

Mittens from step 2

Fig. 1 - *Cutting Diagram for Scarf*

Fig. 2 - *The scarf with the second set of mittens.*

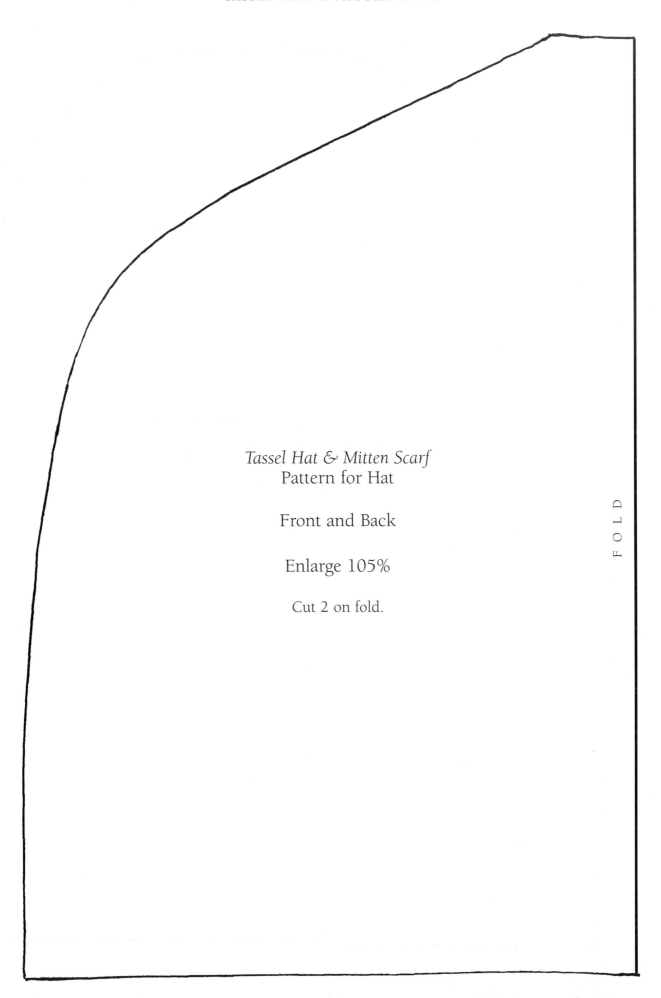

Tassel Hat & Mitten Scarf
Pattern for Hat

Front and Back

Enlarge 105%

Cut 2 on fold.

FOLD

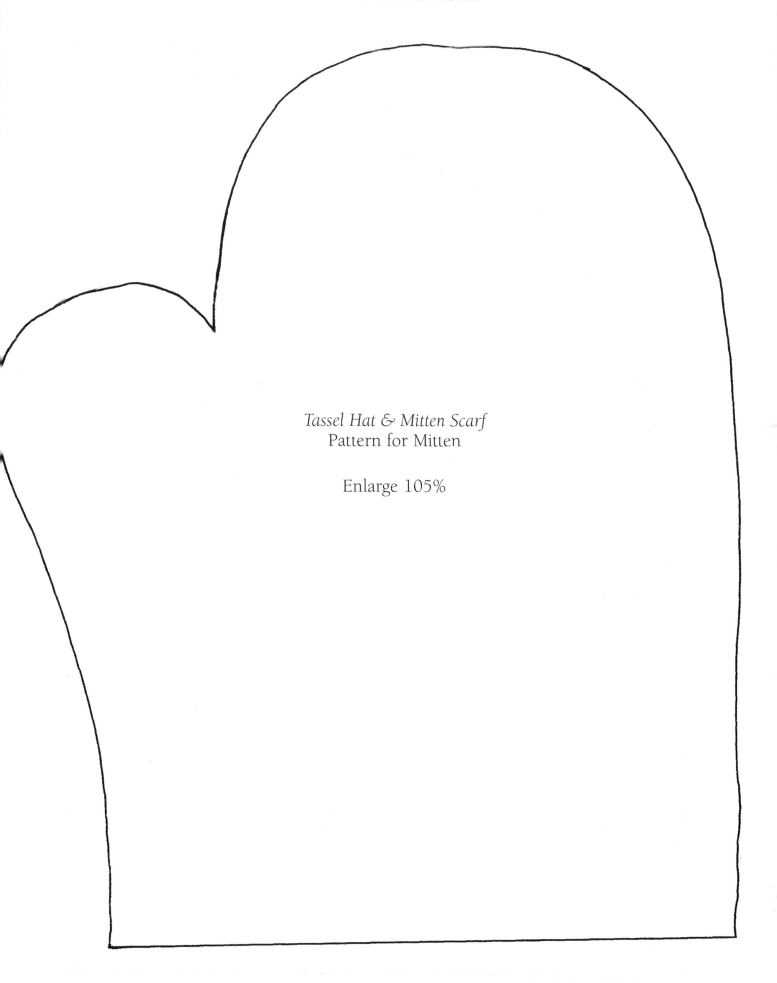

Tassel Hat & Mitten Scarf
Pattern for Mitten

Enlarge 105%

Little Miss Jacket

For this jacket, I was lucky enough to find several floral print sweaters and a gray sweater with wool yarn flowers. The flowers shrank with the sweater. The front is held together with a purchased frog closure. The one I bought was white (it's next to impossible to find colored ones) so I developed a coloring technique that uses a permanent felt-tip marker. The technique is included in the project instructions.

SUPPLIES
- Felted wool, pieced to fit pattern pieces
- 3-strand wool yarn - Bright blue
- Large eye needle, tapestry or darning
- Dark sewing thread
- Stabilizer
- White frog closure
- Permanent felt-tip marker (to color the frog)
- Rubbing alcohol
- Glass jar

INSTRUCTIONS
Make the Jacket:
1. Enlarge patterns.
2. Cut two ribbed sweater sleeve ends for the jacket sleeve ends.
3. Piece felted wool to fit the patterns, placing the ribbed trim at the ends of the sleeves. Overlap the pieces and machine sew on top with a decorative stitch (or stitches).
4. Cut out the patterns.
5. Overlap shoulder seams and side seams and sew with a decorative machine stitch.
6. Add wool trim or a strip of striped wool on the upper edge of the back pocket. Machine stitch pockets in place—one pocket on right front bottom (Fig. 1) and second pocket on center upper back (Fig. 2).

7. Using yarn and darning or tapestry needle, blanket stitch around all edges of the jacket except the ribbed sleeve ends. Blanket stitch around the pockets and down all overlap lines.

Add Flowers:
1. Cut flowers from wool scraps. See Techniques section for instructions for making flowers.
2. Decorate the flowers with wool yarn stitchery (Fig. 3) or appliques from a sweater (Fig. 4), if you have one with appliques.
3. Hand stitch the flowers to the jacket with matching sewing thread.

Add the Frog:
1. Use a permanent felt-tip marker to color as much of the frog pieces as possible on both top and bottom.
2. Pour some rubbing alcohol in a jar large enough to hold the frog and submerge the frog in the alcohol for about five minutes to blend the color. Remove frog and set aside on a paper towel to dry.
3. Sew the frog to the garment with matching thread. ❀

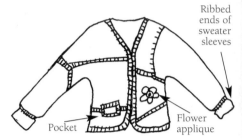

Fig. 1 - *Jacket front*

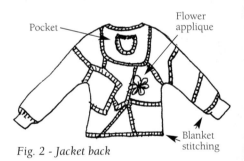

Fig. 2 - *Jacket back*

Fig. 3 - *Flower with yarn center*

Fig. 4 - *Flower with applique center*

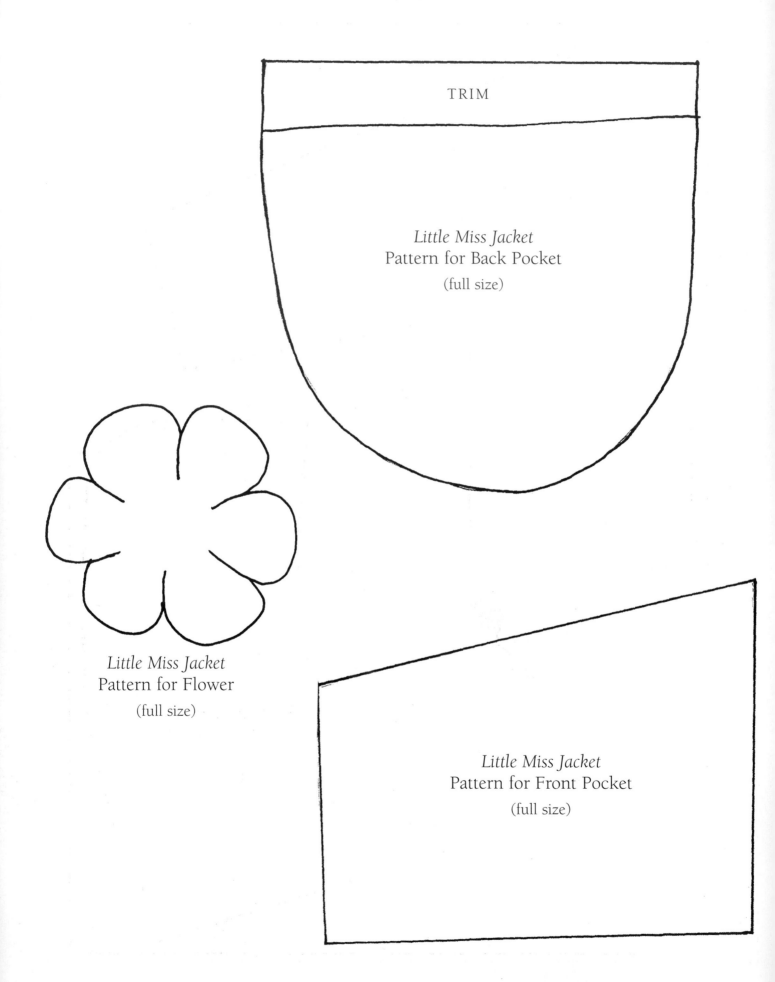

TRIM

Little Miss Jacket
Pattern for Back Pocket
(full size)

Little Miss Jacket
Pattern for Flower
(full size)

Little Miss Jacket
Pattern for Front Pocket
(full size)

19"

Little Miss Jacket
Pattern for Jacket Back

Cut 1 on fold

SLEEVE

F O L D

18-3/4"

= one inch

SLEEVE

Little Miss Jacket Pattern
for Jacket Front

Cut 2

18"

19"

Kitten Shoes & Flat-top Hat

These shoes have elastic backs for a snug fit and cute kitten appliques. The flat-top hat has matching trim for a coordinated look.

Patterns appear on pages 92 and 93.

Kitten Baby Shoes

SUPPLIES
- Felted wool
- Sewing thread and needle
- 6-strand embroidery floss in contrasting color
- Large eye needle, darning or tapestry
- 1/3 yd. trim, 3/4" wide (for the shoe fronts)
- 1/3 yd. elastic, 1/4" wide
- *Optional*: Embroidery floss

For the kitty appliques:
- Small bits of felted wool
- 6-strand embroidery floss - Pink, black

INSTRUCTIONS
1. Choose the appropriate-size pattern.
2. Cut all pieces from felted wool (two fronts, two backs, two bottoms).
3. Cut two pieces of elastic, each 5-1/2" long. Hand sew on the right side of each shoe front 1/8" from the straight edge. (Fig. 1)
4. Cover the elastic with a strip of trim. (Fig. 2)
5. Using the patterns provided, cut out two sets of kitty appliques. Pin one applique to the center front of each shoe and stitch in place. (Fig. 3) (See "Hand Embroidery" in the Basic Techniques section.) The decorative stitches will hold the appliques to the shoes.
6. Embroider the details, using six strands of embroidery floss for all details except the cat's whiskers.(Fig. 4, Fig. 5)
7. Fold the top edge of one shoe back into the inside along the fold line. Whipstitch in place by hand with matching thread and sewing needle. (Fig. 6) Repeat on the other shoe back.
8. Pin the shoe backs to the shoe bottoms with wrong sides together and the raw edges on the outside of the shoe. Use matching thread to baste 1/8" from the edge. (Fig. 7)
9. Pin the shoe fronts to the soles, wrong sides together. (The front will overlap the back.) Baste 1/8" from the outer edges. (Fig. 8)
10. Use 6-strand floss to sew all the way around the shoe.(Fig. 8) ❈

Hat instructions on page 92.

Fig. 1 - *Sewing the elastic to the shoe front.*

Fig. 2 - *Adding the trim over the elastic.*

Fig. 3 - *The applique pieces applied.*

Fig. 4 - *Features with pink thread embroidery (ears, nose, mouth)*

Fig. 5 - *Features with black thread embroidery (eyes, space between nose and mouth, whiskers)*

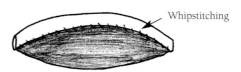

Whipstitching

Fig. 6 - *Folding the top of the shoe back and whipstitching.*

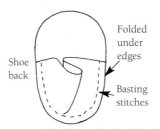

Shoe back

Folded under edges

Basting stitches

Fig. 7 - *Attaching the shoe back.*

Fig. 8 - *Blanket stitching around the edges.*

Flat-top Baby Hat

SUPPLIES
- Felted wool
- Felted wool trim
- 6-strand embroidery floss in contrasting color
- 30" felted wool trim or decorative trim
- Sewing thread to match wool
- Tapestry needle

INSTRUCTIONS
1. Enlarge the pattern for the top. Cut top from felted wool.
2. For the sides, cut two pieces of felted wool, each 10" x 15".
3. With wrong sides together, baste the short ends of the side pieces together, using a 1/4" seam allowance. See Fig. 1.
4. With wrong sides together, pin the top of the hat to the sides. Baste 1/4" from the edge. See Fig. 2.
5. Pin the wool trim to the bottom of the hat on the underside. Fold up the bottom of the hat so the trim shows.
6. Blanket stitch around the top of the hat, down the sides, and around the bottom, attaching the trim. Use six strands of embroidery floss and tapestry needle, spacing the stitches 1/4" apart. See the Basic Techniques section for blanket stitching instructions. ❁

Fig. 1 - Seaming the side pieces.

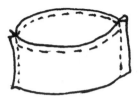

Fig. 2 - Seaming the top piece.

FOLD

Flat-Top Baby Hat
Pattern

Enlarge 200%

Cut 1 on fold

Patterns for Kitten Shoes and Puppy Shoes

Instructions for Kitten Shoes on page 90.
Instructions for Puppy Shoes on page 94.

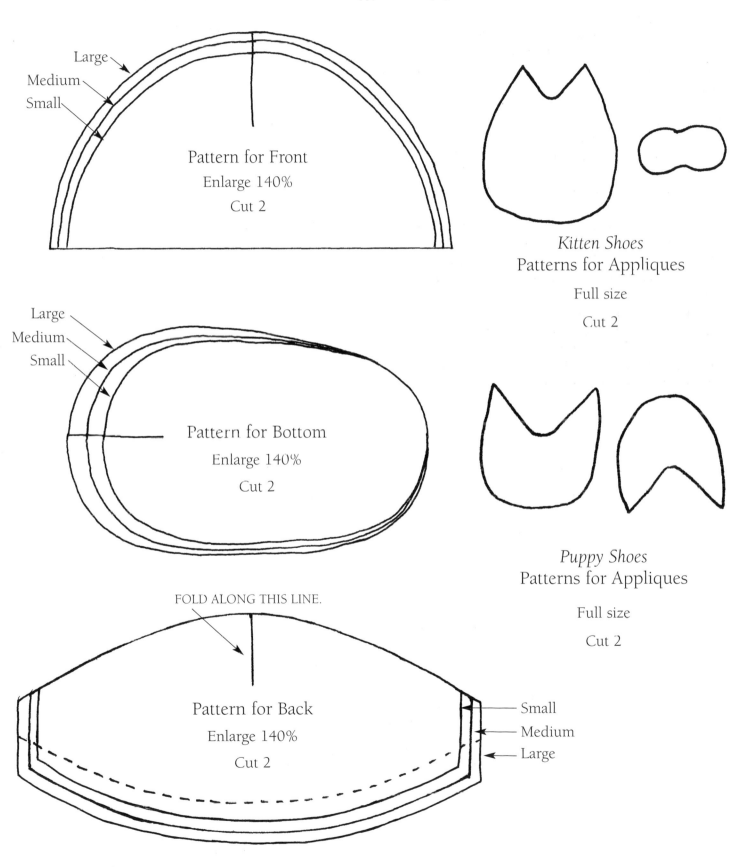

Large
Medium
Small

Pattern for Front
Enlarge 140%
Cut 2

Kitten Shoes
Patterns for Appliques

Full size

Cut 2

Large
Medium
Small

Pattern for Bottom
Enlarge 140%
Cut 2

Puppy Shoes
Patterns for Appliques

Full size

Cut 2

FOLD ALONG THIS LINE.

Pattern for Back
Enlarge 140%
Cut 2

Small
Medium
Large

Puppy Shoes & Pointed-top Hat

Using the same sweaters to make more than one item ensures a coordinated look. Here, the pointed-top hat and the baby shoes, which are trimmed with striped bands and puppy appliques, share common origins.

Patterns appear on pages 93 and 96.

Puppy Baby Shoes

SUPPLIES
- Felted wool
- Sewing thread and needle
- 6-strand embroidery floss in contrasting color
- Large eye needle, tapestry or darning
- 2 contrast strips of felt, 3/4" wide (for the shoe fronts)
- 1/3 yd. elastic, 1/4" wide
- *Optional:* Embroidery floss

For the puppyy appliques:
- Small bits of felted wool
- 6-strand embroidery floss - Red, black

INSTRUCTIONS
1. Choose the appropriate-size pattern.
2. Cut all pieces from felted wool (two fronts, two backs, two bottoms).
3. Cut two pieces of elastic, each 5-1/2" long. Hand sew on the right side of each shoe front 1/8" from the straight edge. (Fig. 1)
4. Cover the elastic with a strip of contrasting felt. Edge the strip with blanket stitching, using six strands of floss and tapestry or darning needle. (Fig. 2)
5. Using the patterns provided, cut out two sets of puppy appliques. Pin one applique to the center front of each shoe and stitch in place. (Fig. 3) (See "Hand Embroidery" in the Basic Techniques section.) The decorative stitches will hold the appliques to the shoes.
6. Satin stitch the puppy's tongue with red floss using a tapestry needle. (Fig. 3)
7. Embroider the remaining puppy features with black floss, using six strands of embroidery floss. (Fig. 4)
8. Fold the top edge of one shoe back into the inside along the fold line. Whipstitch in place by hand with matching thread. (Fig. 5) Repeat on the other shoe back.

continue on page 96

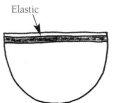
Fig. 1 - Sewing the elastic to the shoe front.

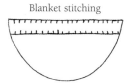
Fig. 2 - Adding a felted strip over the elastic and blanket stitching.

Fig. 3 - Applique puppy pieces and red thread embroidery (tongue) in place.

Fig. 4 - Black thread embroidery (eyes, nose, space between nose and mouth, whiskers).

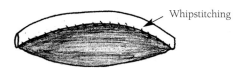
Fig. 5 - Folding the top of the shoe back and whipstitching.

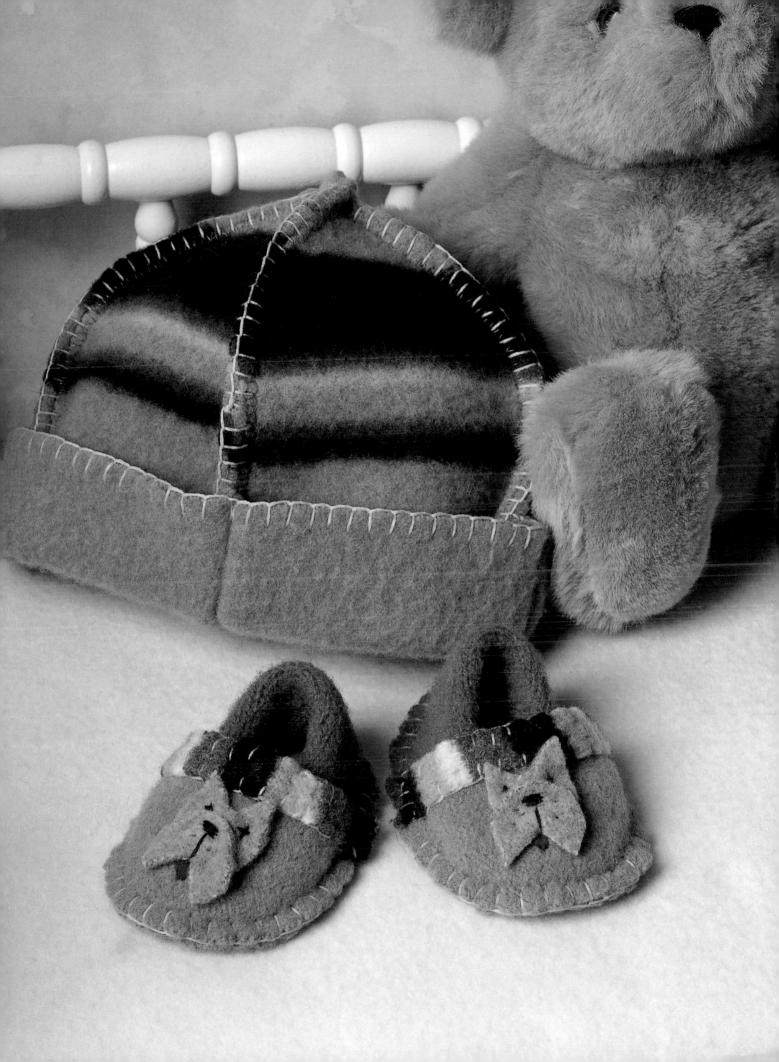

continued from page 94

9. Pin the shoe backs to the shoe bottoms with wrong sides together and the raw edges on the outside of the shoe. Use matching thread to baste 1/8" from the edge. (Fig. 6)

10. Pin the shoe fronts to the soles, wrong sides together. (The front will overlap the back.) Baste 1/8" from the outer edges. (Fig. 7)

11. Use 6-strand floss to sew all the way around the shoe. (Fig. 7) ❀

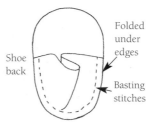

Fig. 6 - *Attaching the shoe back.*

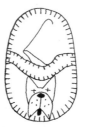

Fig. 7 - *Blanket stitching around the edges.*

Pointed-top Baby Hat

SUPPLIES
- Felted wool
- Contrasting 6-strand embroidery floss
- Stabilizer
- Tapestry needle

INSTRUCTIONS
1. Enlarge the pattern.
2. Cut four of the pattern from felted wool.
3. With two pieces wrong sides together and stabilizer between the two pieces, machine stitch a 1/4" seam starting 1/4" from the point.
4. Do the same with the other two pieces.
5. Sew the two sides together. (The four pieces form the hat.)
6. Using six strands of embroidery floss and a tapestry needle, blanket stitch down each seam and around the bottom edge. See the Techniques section for blanket stitching instructions.
7. Fold up the bottom to make the cuff. ❀

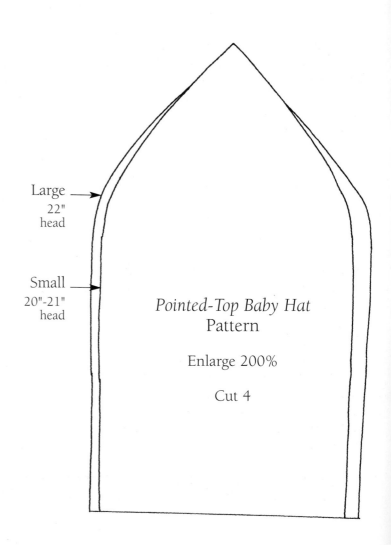

Large
22"
head

Small
20"-21"
head

Pointed-Top Baby Hat
Pattern

Enlarge 200%

Cut 4

Gray Slouch Bag

This bag is made from a single felted sweater. The bottom ribbing of the sweater forms the fold-over flap, which is trimmed with silver medallions.

SUPPLIES
- Grey felted wool sweater, pullover style
- Black sewing thread
- 5 silver medallions (recycled belt parts or conchos)
- 2 black leather handles with silver rings

INSTRUCTIONS
1. Place sweater upside down on your work surface. Cut sweater as shown in Fig. 1.
2. Turn sweater so right sides are together. Stitch across the cut open end (not the end with the ribbing). Turn.
3. Sew 5 medallions or conchos to one side of the ribbed flap. (This side will be the back.)
4. From the scraps of the sweater, cut two strips, each 14" long and 2-1/2" wide.
5. Make four cuts 4" long on each end of each strip to make fringe.
6. Fold each strip in half over the rings of one handle. Position the strips and handle on the side of the bag without the medallions. Machine sew a square below the rings to attach them. See Fig. 2.
7. From the scraps of the sweater, cut two more strips, each 1" wide and 6" long. Fold them over the rings of the other handle and sew them to the back of the bag, using the same spacing you used for the front handles.
8. Fold the ribbing to the front of the back to make the flap. ✻

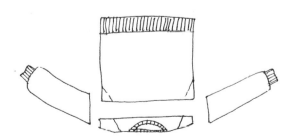

Fig. 1 - Cutting Diagram

Fig. 2 - Attaching the handle on the front of the bag.

Flowered Hat & Scarf

The multicolored scarf has ribbed ruffles and cross-stitch trim, which also accents the hat. Color-coordinated flowers adorn both items.

Patterns appear on page 101.

Hat with Turned-up Brim

SUPPLIES
- Solid-color felted wool (The felted wool should be thick and sturdy so the brim will hang properly.)
- Felted wool flower (Instructions follow.)
- Sewing thread (matching color)
- Sewing needle
- Wool yarn (contrasting color)
- Tapestry needle

INSTRUCTIONS
1. Enlarge patterns.
2. Cut out the brim piece (on the fold) and the top piece from felted wool. Measure the circumference of the top piece 1/4" inside the edge. Cut out the side piece from felted wool. Cut it 4-1/2" wide, with the width being the measurement of the top piece plus 1/4". This is the side piece.
3. Make a tube with the side piece with the right side out. Overlap 1/4" and hand sew the overlapped seam. (Fig. 1) Divide the tube into four equal sections and mark with pins.
4. With right sides out, pin the top of the hat to the side piece, lining up the front, back, and sides. Hand sew 1/4" from the edges. (Fig. 2)
5. Overlap the ends of hat brim and stitch together.
6. With all right sides of the hat to the outside, line up the back seam of brim with the back seam of the side piece. Pin the side piece on the outside of the inner edge of the brim with the inner edge of the brim to the inside of the side piece. They will overlap. See Fig. 3. Sew together with sewing thread.
7. Using two strands of wool yarn and a tapestry needle, stitch around brim of hat, crossing the threads on the edge of the brim. (See the Techniques section for single cross stitch instructions.)
8. Using two strands of wool yarn, stitch where the top joins the side piece with crossed threads on the edge.
9. Using two strands of wool yarn, cross stitch the part where the side piece joins the brim through all layers.

10. Make the flower, using the instructions that follow on page 100.
11. Fold up the brim at the front of the hat and sew the flower to the front of the hat brim. ✿

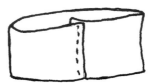

Fig. 1 - Seam in the side piece.

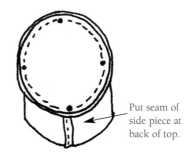

Put seam of side piece at back of top.

Fig. 2 - Join the top piece to the side piece.

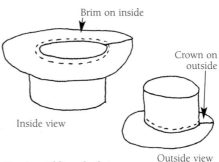

Brim on inside

Crown on outside

Inside view

Outside view

Fig. 3 - Adding the brim.

Scarf with Ribbed Ruffles
SUPPLIES
- Felted wool strips, 6" wide (Use the hat color and complementary colors.)
- Scraps of red and purple felted wool
- Strip of striped wool, 1/4" x 11"
- Felted ribbing, 27" long (from bottom of sweater the hat was made of)
- 3-strand wool yarn - 1 skein violet, scraps of light blue
- Sewing thread to match the felted wool pieces
- Sewing needle
- Tapestry needle

INSTRUCTIONS
1. Join the pieces of wool to make a scarf, overlapping each piece over the previous piece. Don't try to keep lines straight—curves and angles add interest to the scarf. Using matching sewing thread, secure all overlapping pieces with hidden stitches on both sides of the scarf.
2. Cut the 27" piece of ribbing into two equal pieces (each 13-1/2" long). Sew each into a tube by folding in half, right sides together, and sewing the ends. Turn to the right side.
3. Use matching sewing thread to slightly gather the top edge of each ribbed tube. Slide a tube on each end of the scarf and sew the gathered edges to attach them to the scarf.
4. Make the flower, following the instructions for the Hat Flower. **Note:** The flower on the scarf is smaller. Sew the flower to the scarf.
5. Use a cross stitch and two strands of violet wool yarn and a tapestry needle to stitch all the joined edges. See Fig. 1. (You will need to go all around the ribbing at each end.) TIP: When stitching the front side of the scarf, just slightly catch the wool on the back of the scarf - don't go all the way through to the back. Likewise, when stitching the back of the scarf, be careful not to go all the way through to the front.
6. *Option:* If, after finishing the scarf, you notice a moth hole (as I did), make a decorative eyelet out of it. See Fig. 2.

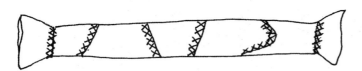

Fig. 1 - Pieced scarf example with cross stitching.

Fig. 2 - A decorative eyelet around a small moth hole.

Flowers for Hat & Scarf
SUPPLIES
- Red felted wool (for outer petal)
- Purple felted wool (for inner petal)
- Striped strip of felted wool, 3/8" x 14", cut across the stripes (for the flower center)
- 3-strand wool yarn - Purple
- Tapestry needle
- Sewing needle and dark thread

INSTRUCTIONS
1. Enlarge patterns as instructed.
2. Cut out outer petal from red felted wool.
3. Cut out inner petal from purple felted wool. Center it on the red flower.
4. Using two strands of wool yarn and a tapestry needle, straight stitch around the edge of the purple petal to attach it to the red petal, placing the stitches 1/4" apart and making them 1/4" long. See Fig. 1.
5. Coil the striped strip of wool and sew together with hidden stitches.
6. Sew the coil to the center of the flower. ✺

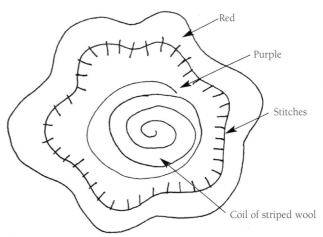

Red

Purple

Stitches

Coil of striped wool

Fig. 1 - Flower diagram

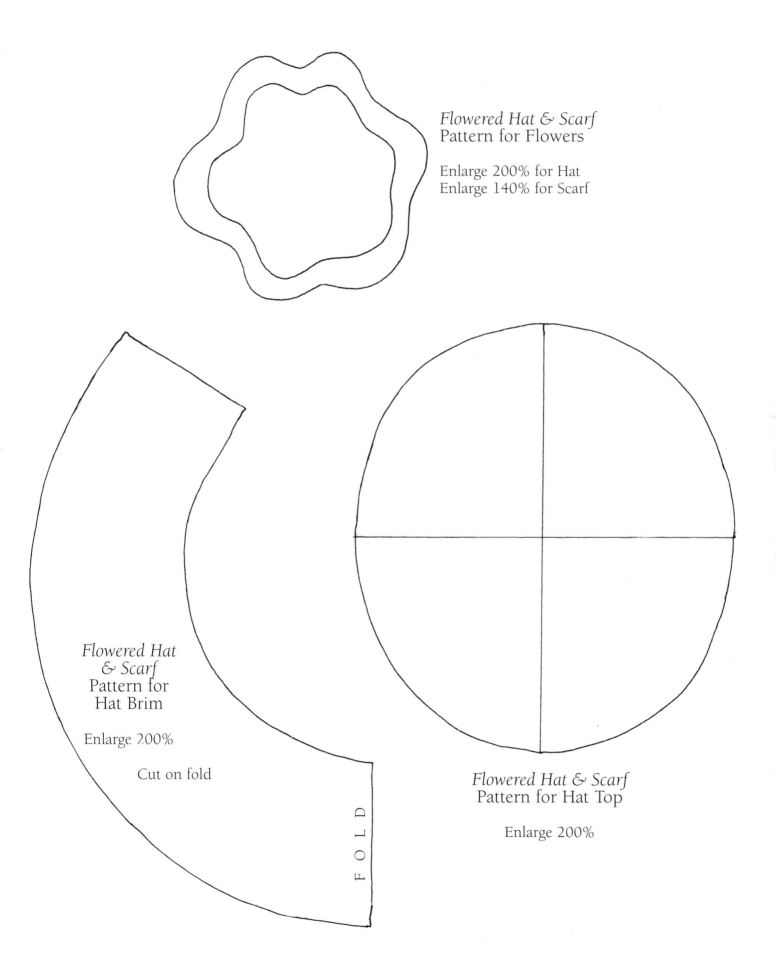

Flowered Hat & Scarf
Pattern for Flowers

Enlarge 200% for Hat
Enlarge 140% for Scarf

*Flowered Hat
& Scarf*
Pattern for
Hat Brim

Enlarge 200%

Cut on fold

FOLD

Flowered Hat & Scarf
Pattern for Hat Top

Enlarge 200%

Turtleneck Doggie Sweater

Keep your furry friend warm on wintry days and nights with a felted wool sweater. Felted sweater sleeves with ribbed sleeve ends work well for small dogs; larger dogs might require a sweater body with a ribbed bottom. The ribbed part from the sweater forms the turtleneck.

SUPPLIES

- Felted wool sweater with ribbing (1 sleeve for a small dog, body for larger dog)
- Sewing thread to match
- Tape measure

INSTRUCTIONS

These instructions are written for using a sweater sleeve to make a doggie sweater. These would work only for small dogs.

1. Measure around your dog's neck. Check the size of the sleeve's ribbed cuff to determine correct size.

2. Measure your dog's rib cage (or around the widest part of the dog's upper body). Check to see if the body of the sleeve will accommodate this measurement.

3. Measure your dog from the neck to the base of the tail. This is how long the sleeve should be from where the ribbing joins the sleeve to the end.

4. To determine how to place the holes for the dog's front legs, measure the distance from the neck to the legs, and how far apart the legs are. To determine the size of the holes, measure around upper part of the dog's front legs. With scissors, cut holes to accommodate the legs.

5. From remaining parts of the sweater, cut two strips to make "sleeves" for the dog's front legs, each 2" x 10". (You may not need the entire 10".)

6. Turn the dog sweater inside out. Pin a dog sleeve strip to each leg opening. Cut off extra length. Sew a seam where the ends meet on each sleeve. Sew to the openings, with the seams inside the sweater. Turn right side out.

7. Trim the sweater to fit longer on top (the dog's back) and shorter on the bottom (the dog's belly). Fold the ribbing to form the turtleneck. ✿

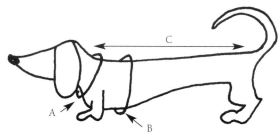

Fig. 1 - Measuring your dog.
  Neck (a)
  Rib cage (b)
  Length of body (c)

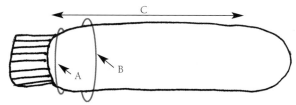

Fig. 2 - Applying the measurements to the sweater sleeve.

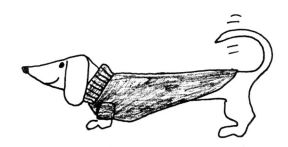

Starburst Hat

An eight-pointed star forms the brim of this whimsical hat. Using a single solid-color sweater keeps the focus on the star shape.

Patterns appear on pages 108 and 109.

SUPPLIES
- Felted wool
- Sewing thread to match
- Stabilizer

INSTRUCTIONS
1. Overlap the ends of the two top lining pieces 1/2" and topstitch to seam together. (Fig. 1)
2. With wrong sides together, lay the top on the top lining, aligning the points. Topstitch 1/2" from the outer edge. Trim the seam allowance to 1/4".
3. With right sides together, sew the two short ends of the band together, using a 1/2" seam allowance. Press the seams open. Topstitch on either side of both seams to secure the seam allowances.
4. Fold the band in half with the wrong sides together. Sew the raw edges together 1/4" from edge. (Fig. 2)
5. Pin the band to the opening of the top lining with right sides together, aligning the two seams on the band with the two seams on the top lining. (Fig. 3)
6. Stitch the seam, using a 1/4" seam allowance. ❉

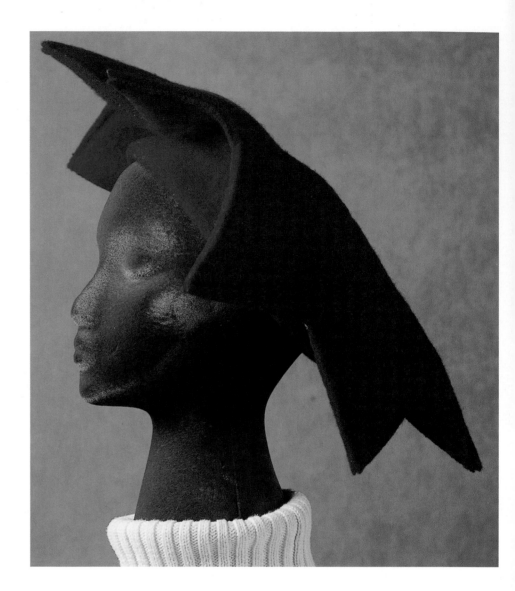

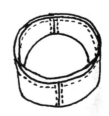

Fig. 1 - Stitching the seams in the top lining.

Fig. 2 - Constructing the band.

Fig. 3 - Attaching the band to the top lining.

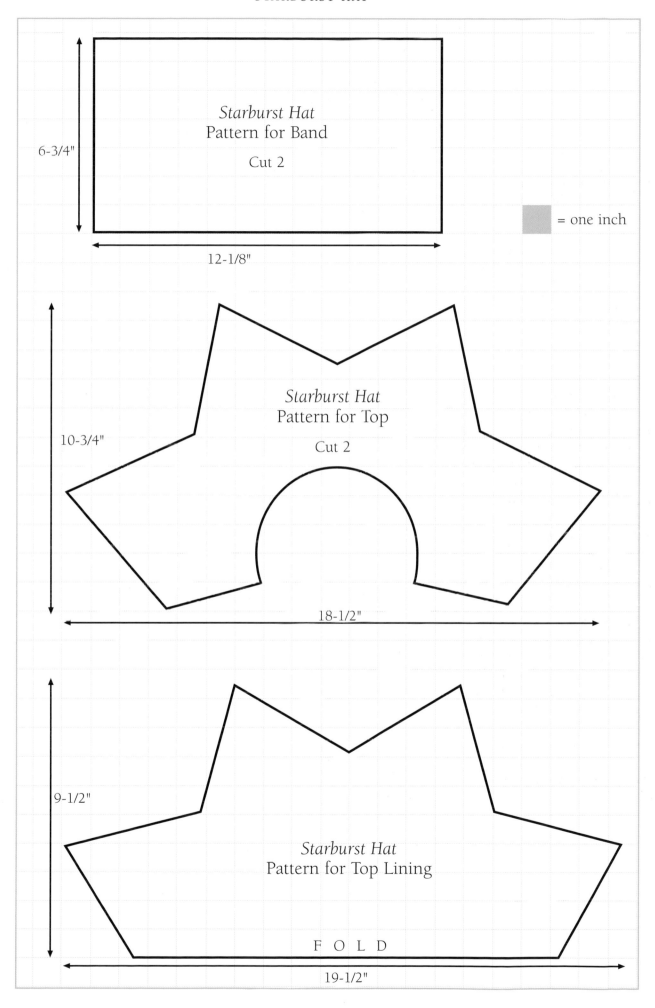

Starburst Hat
Pattern for Band

Cut 2

6-3/4"

12-1/8"

= one inch

Starburst Hat
Pattern for Top

Cut 2

10-3/4"

18-1/2"

Starburst Hat
Pattern for Top Lining

9-1/2"

F O L D

19-1/2"

Zig-zag Bag with Buttons

A zig-zag accented with blanket stitches and buttons decorates this simple bag.

SUPPLIES

- 1 medium blue felted wool sweater, cardigan-style
- 2 purse handles with rings attached
- 3 decorative buttons
- 6-strand embroidery floss *or* wool yarn - Lime green
- Felted wool sleeve from a striped sweater (for flower)
- Sewing thread (to match felted wool sweater)
- Stabilizer

INSTRUCTIONS

1. Lay felted cardigan, button side up, on a flat surface. Leave it buttoned. Cut the sweater, using Fig. 1 as a guide.
2. Remove the buttons. Overlap the fronts with the buttonhole side on the bottom. Cut the front side that's on top in a zig-zag pattern. See the Pattern for Cutting the Zig-zag and Fig. 2.
3. Use 6-strand embroidery floss or yarn to sew the zig-zag edge to the other side of the front, using a blanket stitch. Sew through both front layers so the front opening is sewn closed.
4. Turn the bag inside out. Machine sew across the open bottom, using stabilizer under the seam. Turn right side out.
5. Turn under all the raw edges around the top of the bag and machine stitch to secure, again using stabilizer.
6. Pull the extensions on the top of the bag through the loops of the handles. Fold the extensions to the inside and sew in place. (Fig. 3)
7. Turn the bag right side out. Decorate with buttons along the zig-zag as shown in the photo.
8. Make a flower and pin or sew to one side of the front. See the section called Making Flowers for instructions. ❀

--- Cut on these lines.

Fig. 1 - Cutting diagram for the basic shape.

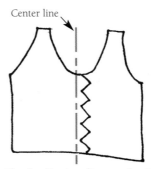

Center line

Fig. 2 - Cutting diagram for the zig-zag detail.

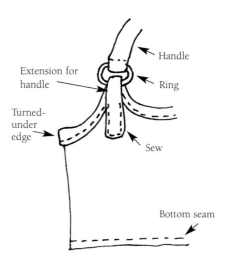

Handle

Extension for handle

Ring

Turned-under edge

Sew

Bottom seam

Fig. 3 - Inside view of bag with stitching.

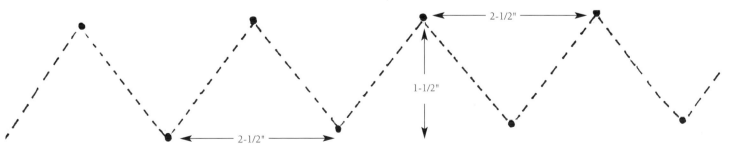

2-1/2"

1-1/2"

2-1/2"

Pattern for Cutting the Zig-zag

Striped Bag with Zipper Bow

Zippers, colored safety pins, and buttons decorate a bag made from a felted striped sweater. Choose zippers in a color to match one of the stripes on your bag.

SUPPLIES

- Felted wool striped sweater, pullover-style
- 3 decorative buttons
- 3 backing buttons
- Safety pins, 1-1/4" long - 24 blue, 24 purple
- Colored zippers, one 24" (for the bow) plus others whose lengths, added together, are slightly longer than twice as long as the width of the bag
- Sewing thread (to match bag)
- 1/2 yd. lining fabric
- 1/2 yd. heavyweight double-sided fusible interfacing

INSTRUCTIONS

Make the Bag:

1. Cut the sweater, using Fig. 1 as a guide.
2. Refold the cutout part of the sweater with one handle in front and one in the back. (Fig. 2)
3. Turn the bag inside out and sew across the bottom. (Fig. 3)
4. Make rounded handles by turning the raw edges in and sewing. (Fig. 3) Turn the raw edges along the top to the inside and stitch.
5. Cut out two closure flaps, using the pattern provided. With right sides together, sew around three sides, using a 1/4" seam allowance and leaving the straight end open for turning. Turn right side out.
6. Make a buttonhole on the curved point of the closure flap. (See "Buttonholes & Buttons" in the Basic Techniques section).
7. Turn in the raw edges on the open end. Position the flap on the outside center back of the bag 2" from the top. Sew across the bottom and up 1" on each side of the flap.
8. Sew one decorative button on the front to hold the closure flap. (See "Buttonholes & Buttons" in the Basic Techniques section.)
9. Sew two decorative buttons on the front of the purse.

Add the Lining:

1. Measure the height and width of the bag. Cut a piece of lining fabric as wide as the bag and twice as long as the height plus 1".
2. Cut a piece of interfacing smaller in each dimension than the lining (e.g., if the lining is 16" x 13", the interfacing should be 14" x 12".)
3. Place the interfacing in the center of the wrong side of the lining fabric piece. Fold over all the edges and baste. (Fig. 4)
4. Fold the interfaced lining in half so the lining side is on the inside and the interfacing side is on the outside. Sew down the sides. (Fig. 5)
5. Insert the lining in the bag and sew in place along the top of the lining. See Fig. 6.

Finish:

1. Pin the safety pins along one of the stripes of the sweater, alternating blue and purple pins and placing them about 2" from the bottom of the bag and 1/2" apart.
2. Thread the zippers through the safety pins, stitching them to secure where they overlap and placing the end with the tab pull on top.
3. Make a bow with the 24" zipper. Sew it on the front on top of the zippers around the bag. ✱

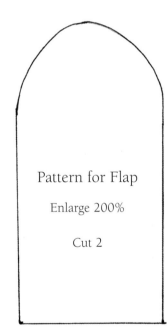

Pattern for Flap

Enlarge 200%

Cut 2

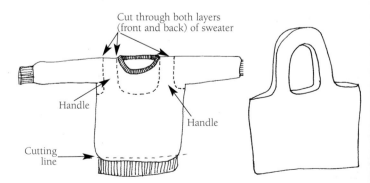

Cut through both layers (front and back) of sweater

Handle

Handle

Cutting line

Fig. 1 - Cutting diagram.

Fig. 2 - How to refold the bag.

108

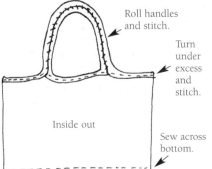

Roll handles and stitch.

Turn under excess and stitch.

Inside out

Sew across bottom.

Fig. 3 - Inside view of straps and bottom seam.

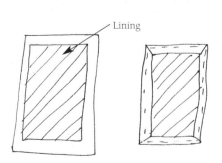

Lining

Fig. 4 - Adding the interfacing to the lining piece.

Fig. 5 - Constructing the lining.

Liner

Fig. 6 - Attaching the lining inside the bag.

V-Top Shoulder Bag

This bag—cut from a single sweater—swings from long straps and is decorated with yarn and two felted wool flowers. The platform bottom, made from cardboard or mat board covered with felted wool, provides a sturdy base.

SUPPLIES
- Felted wool sweater, pullover-style
- Double handles with rings attached, 29" long
- Heavy cardboard *or* mat board, 2-1/4" wide and as long as the bag is wide
- Sewing thread (to match sweater)
- 3 decorative yarns, each 40" long
- Two felted wool flowers
- Stabilizer

INSTRUCTIONS
1. Cut out the bag from the sweater, using Fig. 1 as a guide.
2. Use a zig-zag stitch to sew three strands of decorative yarn around the purse. (Fig. 2) TIPS: It's much easier to do this while the bottom of the bag is still open. Always use stabilizer when machine stitching.
3. Turn the bag inside out and sew across the bottom. (Fig. 3)
4. Turn under all raw edges along the top of the purse and sew. (Fig. 3)
5. Pull the top ends through the rings of the handles and turn to the inside. Adjust them, making sure they are even, and sew the ends to secure. (Fig. 4)
6. Sew the flowers on the front of the bag. See the Making Flowers section for instructions.
7. Cut the cardboard or mat board piece to fit the bottom of the bag. Cut two pieces of felted wool the size of the cardboard or mat board plus 1/4" on all sides. Sandwich the cardboard or mat board between the pieces of wool, right sides out, and sew all around the edges to make the platform bottom. (Fig. 5)
8. Insert the platform bottom in the bag and stitch to secure in place. ❁

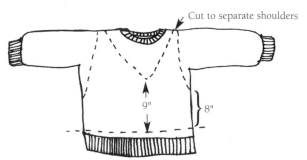

Fig. 1 - Cutting diagram.

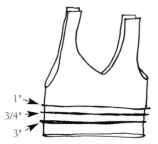

Fig. 2 - Placement diagram for yarn trim.

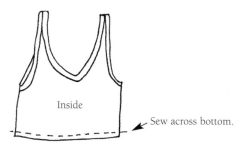

Fig. 3 - Inside view of top edge finishing and bottom seam.

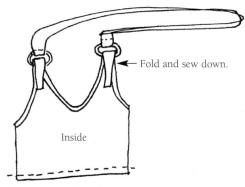

Fig. 4 - Attaching the straps.

Fig. 5 - Making the platform bottom.

Easy Tote with Embroidered Leaves

This simple tote could be used as a purse, a briefcase, or a shopping bag or to carry knitting or crocheting projects.

SUPPLIES
- Felted wool sweater, pullover-style
- 2 bamboo handles, 15"
- Sewing thread (to match sweater)
- 1 yd. brown yarn
- Brown thread (to match yarn)
- 18" very heavy green yarn
- Felted wool flower
- 6-strand embroidery thread - Dark green, medium green, light green
- Chalk
- Tapestry needle

INSTRUCTIONS
1. Cut out the tote, using Fig. 1 as a guide.
2. Using hand stitches or a zig-zag stitch on the sewing machine, couch a piece of brown yarn all around the tote 3" above the bottom edge.
3. Using whip stitches 1/4" apart, couch the heavy green yarn on the tote to make the stem with one strand of dark green embroidery floss. (Fig. 2)
4. With chalk, draw two leaves along the stem, using the pattern provided.
5. Use a chain stitch and dark green six-strand floss to embroider the leaf stems and outlines of the leaves. (Fig. 3)
6. Again chain stitching, fill in half of each leaf with light green and half with medium green. Start near the outline and work rows toward the center, making the last row on each leaf half along the center vein. (Fig. 4)
7. Turn the bag inside out. Sew the bottom seam. Turn right side out.
8. Fold the top tabs over the bamboo handles. Be sure they are even, then sew the ends of the tabs on the inside.
9. Sew the flower at the end of the stem, using the photo as a guide for placement. See the Making Flowers section for instructions. ❀

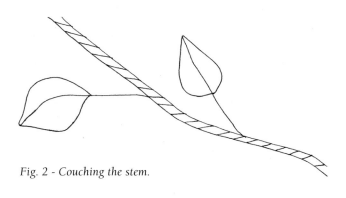

Fig. 1 - Cutting diagram.

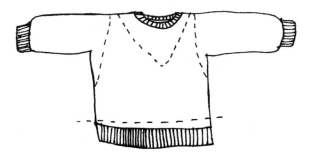

Fig. 2 - Couching the stem.

Fig. 3 - Chain stitching the leaf outlines.

Pattern for Leaves

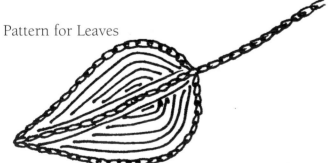

Fig. 4 - Stitching diagram for filling in the leaf shapes.

Plaid Easy Tote

This tote, made from a plaid sweater, is constructed like the Easy Tote with Embroidered Leaves.

SUPPLIES

- Plaid felted wool sweater, pullover-style
- Assorted yarns (in complementary colors)
- Bamboo handles
- Sewing thread (to match or blend with the plaid and yarns)
- Felted wool flower

INSTRUCTIONS

1. Cut out the bag, using Fig. 1 from the Easy Tote with Embroidered Leaves
   as a guide.
2. Using zig-zag machine stitches, sew the yarns to the bag along the lines of the plaid, going up and down as well as around.
3. Using the patterns provided, cut out three leaves from the sweater scraps.
4. Position the leaves on the bag in a cluster, using the photo as a guide, and stitch in place along the center of each.
5. Turn the bag inside out. Sew the bottom seam. Turn right side out.
6. Fold the top tabs over the bamboo handles. Be sure they are even, then sew the ends of the tabs on the inside.
7. Sew a flower at the center of the leaf cluster. See the Making Flowers section for instructions. ❋

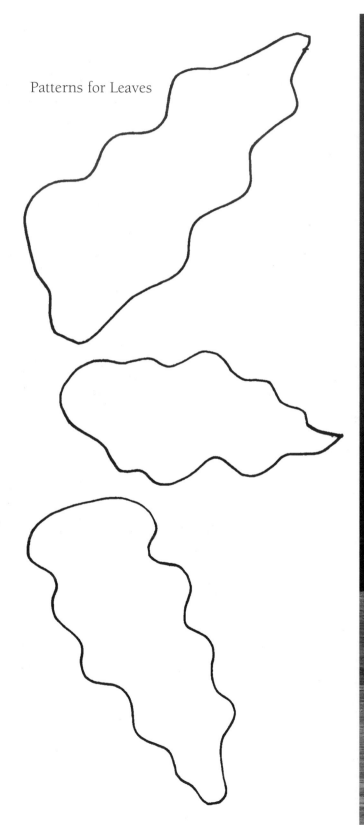

Patterns for Leaves

Embroidered Bag

To make this bag, I felted an embroidered gray cardigan sweater. The silver buckle and buttons are simple, sophisticated accents.

SUPPLIES
- Embroidered felted wool sweater, cardigan-style
- 3 decorative silver buttons
- Silver buckle
- Black sewing thread
- 2 magnetic closures
- Stabilizer
- Sewing needle

INSTRUCTIONS
1. Remove the buttons from the sweater.
2. Overlap the fronts with the buttonholes on the outside and sew closed by hand, inside and outside. (Fig. 1)
3. Cut out the purse shape, using Fig. 2 as a guide. Cut out a 3" x 14" strip for the flap.
4. Refold purse so the sweater's center front and center back are at the sides. See Fig. 3.
5. Pin the strip you cut for the flap to the center back of the bag, aligning the end of the strip with the bottom edge of the bag.
6. Turn the bag inside out and machine sew the bottom seam, including the end of the flap, using a 1/4" seam allowance. Be sure to use stabilizer.
7. Turn the bag right side out. Turn under the edges of the handles, forming the rounded handles. Sew the handles closed. Turn under the top edges to the inside and sew.
8. Sew three decorative buttons on the side of the bag (the former center front). (Fig. 3)
9. Hand sew flap to the back of the bag on both sides.
10. Loop the end of the flap through the buckle. Sew close to the buckle to secure. Sew the end of the flap to hold it in place. (Fig. 3)
11. Attach the magnetic closures according to package instructions, placing one side under the flap and the other to the front of the bag so that they align.
12. *Option:* Use some of the scraps from the sweater to make a matching phone pocket. See the Purse Phone Pocket project for instructions. ❁

Fig. 1 - The sweater before cutting.

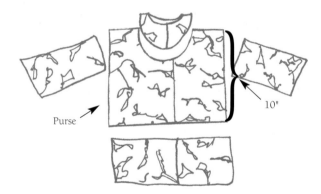

Purse   10"

Fig. 2 - Cutting Diagram

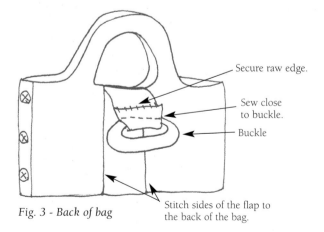

Secure raw edge.

Sew close to buckle.

Buckle

Stitch sides of the flap to the back of the bag.

Fig. 3 - Back of bag

Side view

Beaded Clutch with Strap

This easy-to-make bag uses a decorated piece of colorful felted wool to cover the outside of a purchased shoulder bag, which is used as a liner. You can, of course, change the beading or embroidery to accommodate the particular piece of wool you are using. The bag's strap was replaced with a beaded one; the lobster clasps on each end of the strap make it easily detachable.

SUPPLIES
- Patterned striped felted wool, 13" x 7"
- Black satin bag with zipper closure and shoulder strap, 7" x 6"
- Wool yarns - Coral, turquoise, old gold
- Seed beads - Red, silver-lined lime green, clear turquoise, opaque turquoise
- E beads - Gold, black, red
- Small pony beads - Teal
- Black sewing thread
- Beading needle
- Large eye needle, tapestry or darning

For the strap:
- 1-1/2 yds. flexible beading wire, 0.46 mm
- 2 gold crimp beads, size 1
- 2 gold lobster clasps
- 14 round multi-colored foiled beads, 8 mm
- 44 (approx.) gold rocaille beads
- 16 textured gold beads, 6 mm
- 28 gold beads, 4 mm
- 14 gold round washer-type beads, 6 mm
- Crimping tool

INSTRUCTIONS

Make the Bag:
1. Following the Beading Guide, sew the seed beads, E beads, and pony beads to the right side of the felted wool, using the beading needle and black thread.
2. Embroider the wool yarns, following the Embroidery Guide. Use one strand of wool yarn for stitches and tapestry or darning needle.
3. With wrong sides together, fold the beaded and embroidered wool to make a pocket 7" x 6-1/2". Using matching thread, whipstitch the sides closed. Turn right side out.
4. With scissors, cut the shoulder strap off the black satin bag, leaving the two tabs that attached the strap to the bag. (Fig. 1)
5. Push the black bag into the wool envelope. Sew the edges together around the top of the black bag.

Fig. 1 - Cut strap off the black satin bag, leaving the tabs attached.

Make the Beaded Strap:
1. Thread a crimp bead on one end of the wire. Loop the end of the wire through the claw part of one lobster clasp and run the end of the wire back through the crimp bead. Crimp the bead.
2. String the beads on the wire, using Fig. 2 as a guide.
3. Finish the other end with the other clasp and crimp bead. ❁

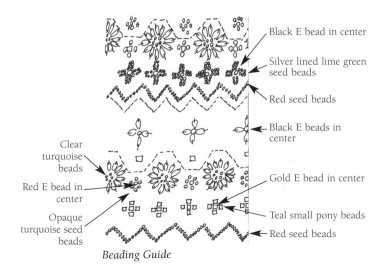

Black E bead in center

Silver lined lime green seed beads

Red seed beads

Black E beads in center

Clear turquoise beads

Gold E bead in center

Red E bead in center

Opaque turquoise seed beads

Teal small pony beads

Red seed beads

Beading Guide

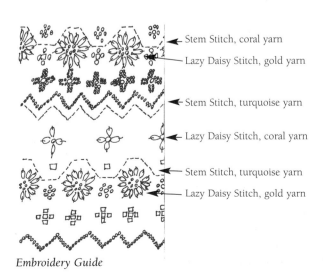

← Stem Stitch, coral yarn

← Lazy Daisy Stitch, gold yarn

← Stem Stitch, turquoise yarn

← Lazy Daisy Stitch, coral yarn

← Stem Stitch, turquoise yarn

← Lazy Daisy Stitch, gold yarn

Embroidery Guide

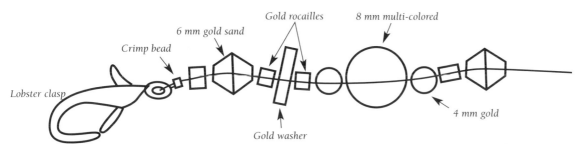

Lobster clasp

Crimp bead

6 mm gold sand

Gold rocailles

Gold washer

8 mm multi-colored

4 mm gold

Fig. 2 - Beading the handle.

Spiral Embroidered Easy Tote

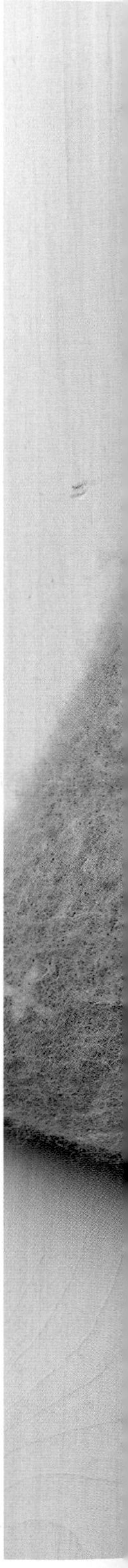

This variation on the Easy Tote was made from a sweater I found that was embroidered with snowflakes. Because the snowflakes were made of wool yarn, they felted when I felted the sweater. If you can't find a sweater with embroidered snowflakes, you can embroider the snowflakes on your sweater with wool yarn before felting for the same effect. I've provided a snowflake pattern below.

SUPPLIES

- Embroidered and felted snowflake sweater, pullover style
- Decorative yarns - Turquoise, white, silver
- Bamboo handles
- Tapestry needle

INSTRUCTIONS

1. Cut out the bag, using Fig. 1 from the Easy Tote with Embroidered Leaves as a guide.
2. Embellish the sweater with chain-stitched spirals, using the decorative yarns. (See the pattern, below.) For information about chain stitching, see "Hand Embroidery" in the Basic Techniques section.
3. Turn the bag inside out. Sew the bottom seam. Turn right side out.
4. Fold the top tabs over the bamboo handles. Be sure they are even, then sew the ends of the tabs on the inside.

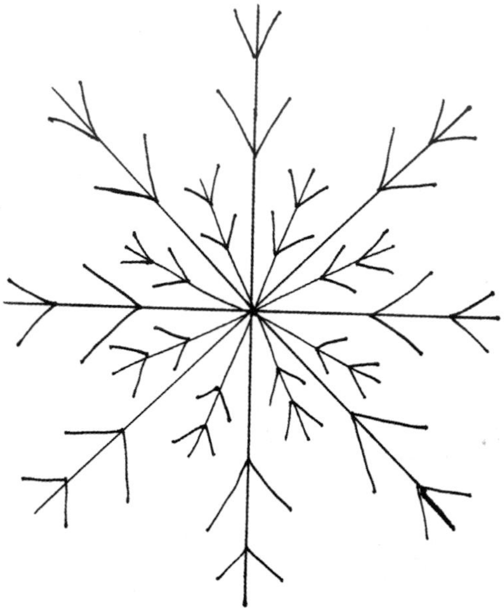

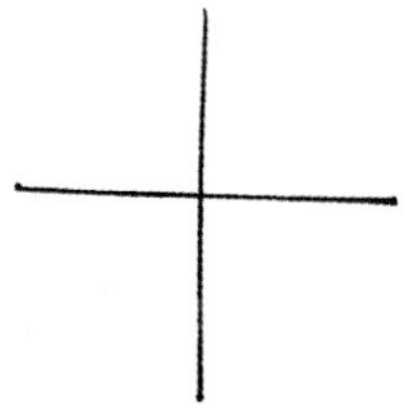

Enlarge Patterns 200%

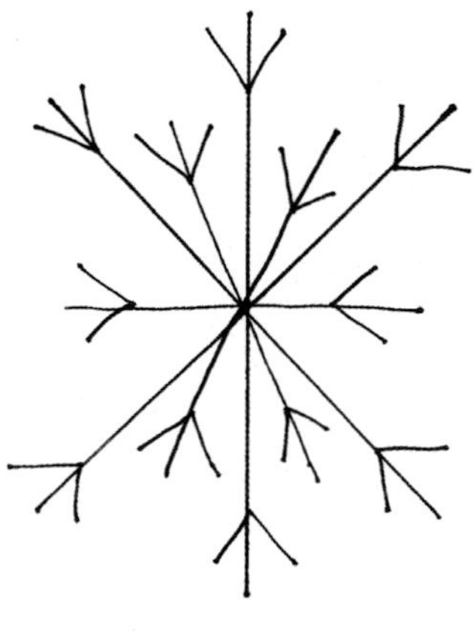

Fancy Flower Easy Tote

This tote, made from a striped sweater, is constructed like the Easy Tote with Embroidered Leaves. It's decorated with novelty yarns and accented with a felted wool flower with ruffled petals.

SUPPLIES

- Felted wool sweater with vertical stripes, pullover style
- Assorted yarns—smooth, glittery, fuzzy, bulky—in 24" lengths
- Bamboo handles
- Scraps of felted wool (for flower), 2" x 12", 3" x 18"
- Dark sewing thread
- Sewing needle

INSTRUCTIONS

1. Cut out the bag, using Fig. 1 from the Easy Tote with Embroidered Leaves as a guide.
2. Turn the bag inside out. Sew the bottom seam. Turn right side out.
3. Fold the top tabs over the bamboo handles. Be sure they are even, then sew the ends of the tabs on the inside.
4. With sewing thread, whip stitch the yarns to the bag along the vertical stripes. Start all the yarns at the top on the front, then go around the finished bottom and up the other side.
5. Sew the ends of the 3" flower strip together to make a big loop. Gather one edge. Repeat the process on the 2" strip.
6. Gather the strips to make the ruffled flower petals.
7. Sew the smaller petal on top of the larger petal and attach to front of the bag.
8. Use small pieces of the yarns to accent the center of the flower.
8. Sew the flower to the bag, using the photo as a guide for placement. ✿

Cuff Bracelet

SUPPLIES

- Strip of grey felted ribbing from sweater bottom, 14" x 3"
- 2" circle of cranberry felted wool
- Silver metallic shank button, 1-1/4"
- 4 yds. (approx.) orange wool 3-ply yarn
- 1 two-hole button, 1" (for underside - any color)
- Tapestry needle

INSTRUCTIONS

1. Use all 3 plys of yarn to stitch over the edges of the 2" cranberry circle. Make the stitches 1/4" deep and 1/8" apart.

2. Cut the ribbing 1-1/2" wide on one end and 3" wide on the other as indicated in Fig. 1.

3. Roll the cuff around your wrist with the wide end on the bottom and the narrow end on the top. Pin in place. Be sure you can easily take it off and on comfortably.

4. Tack in place 1" from the narrow end. Place the plain two-hole button on the underside with the cranberry circle and shank button on top. Sew all together over the tack. ❂

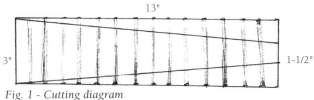

Fig. 1 - Cutting diagram

Button Bracelet

SUPPLIES
- 1 sleeve cuff from a felted wool sweater, 2" wide (ribbed section only)
- 190 (approx.) assorted beads - various shapes and colors
- 30 (approx.) assorted buttons (to match beads)
- Sewing thread (to match cuff)
- 6 yds. black stretchy cord, 0.5 mm
- Sewing needle

INSTRUCTIONS
1. With needle and sewing thread, sew beads as close together as possible along one edge of cuff.
2. Do the same on the other edge of the cuff.
3. Thread the needle with the stretchy cord and sew buttons all along the center of the cuff.
4. *If the cuff fits your arm,* your bracelet is ready to wear. *If the cuff is too loose,* stitch around the center of the cuff several times with stretchy cord, hiding the stitches under the buttons. Pull the cord until it makes the cuff small enough to fit over your hand and stay on your wrist. Knot the cord and trim the end. ❊

Memory Wire Bracelet

SUPPLIES
- Stainless steel memory wire bracelet with 5 loops
- 100 gold-plated E beads
- 100 felted wool pieces, 1/2" square (50 dark red, 50 red)
- Needlenose pliers

INSTRUCTIONS
1. Use pliers to make a loop on one end of the wire.
2. Thread an E bead on the wire.
3. Push the wire through a dark red wool square, add another bead, then a red wool square and a bead. Repeat this sequence to fill the wire and complete the bracelet, ending with a bead.
4. Make a loop on the other end of the wire. ❊